"Eric Ward and Garrett French have put together a solid, easy-to-read link-building primer. The book provides simple explanations and straightforward advice when it comes to building links; chapters are well outlined and flow from point to point. If you are new to link building this book is a great resource for anyone looking for tools, tactics, and case studies to learn from."

—Debra Mastaler, President of alliance-link.com

"Eric Ward has been a thought leader in how to build links the right way since before there even was a right way. His extensive relationship building background mixed with challenging projects has given him insights and methodologies that are advanced and increasingly necessary in today's internet marketing world. He has brought his many years of hard fought experience to the pages of this book, and I heartily recommend it to anyone seeking to grow their skills."

—Bruce Clay, CEO of International SEO firm bruceclay.com, and author of *Search Engine Optimization All-In-One for Dummies*

"Eric Ward pioneered the practice of link building as a marketing channel and continues to be among the thought leaders of the field. His expertise and hands-on experience are virtually unmatched, and I'd recommend his book to anyone who uses links to help grow their business."

—Rand Fishkin, CEO of SEOmoz.org

"Those who want link building done right by the best in the business flock to Eric Ward and count themselves lucky that the maestro isn't booked into the next millennium."

—Jim Sterne, targeting.com, Founder of the eMetrics Marketing Optimization Summit and Founding President and current Chairman of the Digital Analytics Association

"Eric Ward is hands-down the smartest thinker in the space when it comes to link building. I guarantee this book will open up any mental blocks you've had about where to get started and set you on a path to becoming a link magnet."

—Mike Grehan, Publisher of Search Engine Watch and ClickZ.com, Producer SES International, and SEMPO Board of Directors

"If you're in SEO and take your job seriously, you know Eric and Garrett. When Eric and Garrett talk about link building, you listen. The only issue when they talk is—there's too much genius to write it all down. So, when *they* do the writing down for you, you buy the book and read it. Twice. At least. You won't regret it."

—Joost de Valk, Founder and CEO of Yoast.com

"Eric is the undisputed master of quality link building. We've worked together for years and he's frequently surprised me with new insights and little-known, and easily executed, strategies to build our customers' backlink portfolios.

—Richard Stokes, CEO of AdGooroo.com and author of *Mastering Search Advertising—How the Top 3% of Search Advertisers Dominate Google AdWords* and *The Ultimate Guide to Pay-Per-Click Advertising*

Entrepreneur MAGAZINE'S

ULTIMATE

GUIDE TO

LINK
BUILDING

- Build backlinks
- Earn a **higher search engine rank**
- Increase the authority and popularity of your site

ERIC WARD & GARRETT FRENCH

EP
Entrepreneur
PRESS®

Entrepreneur Press, Publisher
Cover Design: Andrew Welyczko
Production and Composition: Eliot House Productions

This publication is designed to provide accurate and authoritative information in regard to the subject matter covered. It is sold with the understanding that the publisher is not engaged in rendering legal, accounting or other professional services. If legal advice or other expert assistance is required, the services of a competent professional person should be sought.

Library of Congress Cataloging-in-Publication Data
Ward, Eric.
      Ultimate guide to link building : build backlinks, earn a higher search engine rank, increase the authority and popularity of your site / by Eric Ward and Garrett French.
      p. cm.
      ISBN-13: 978-1-59918-442-5 (alk. paper)
      ISBN-10: 1-59918-442-7 (alk. paper)
      ebook ISBN: 978-1-61308-180-8
      1. Websites—Design. 2. Website development. I. French, Garrett. II. Title.
TK5105.888.W3615 2013
006.7—dc23   2012037716

Printed in the United States of America

17 16 15 14 13   10 9 8 7 6 5 4 3 2

Contents

Acknowledgments

ERIC WARD

Thank you to my wife Melissa for putting up with the long hours it took to get my company off the ground in the early '90s, for waking me up at 3 A.M. when I'd fallen asleep at the keyboard in the middle of a link-building campaign, and for giving me three beautiful kids along the way. My thanks also to mom and dad, who are surprised I have written a book because there was scant evidence in my academic history to suggest this was a possibility. I always *was* a late bloomer. A huge thanks goes to Garrett French, my co-author, because without him you would not be reading this right now. And finally, thanks to Rich Stokes at AdGooroo, who helped me believe I could do it.

GARRETT FRENCH

First and foremost, I must thank my wife. When I called her years ago from the office parking lot to tell her I'd been laid off, she responded: "Awesome!" She stood by me with zero doubt in the entrepreneurial years that have followed and is the world's best partner and mother.

Rich Ord, founder of iEntry, was my first business mentor. He gave me the keys to an email list of 400,000 ebusiness owners in 2001. That's where I learned about audience, content and market conversations.

J. Donald Robinson, my grandfather, was a computer salesman back when they were mechanical. His voice lights up when we talk business and sales and his belief in me always leaves me rejuvenated.

My industry inspirations are too many to name but I'll give it a quick shot: Eric Ward of course, Debra Mastaler, Wil Reynolds, Darren Shaw, Russ Jones, Andy Beal, Shari Thurow, Ammon Johns, Gianluca Fiorelli, Greg Shuey, Adam Henige, Eric Covino, Bill Slawski, Don Rhoades, Tony Spencer, Jeremy Bencken, Paul May, Paddy Moogan, Ross Hudgens, Lyndon Antcliff, Hugo Guzman, Terry Van Horne, Shaun Anderson, Patrick Gavin, Dan Thies, Tom Demers, Melanie Nathan, Ken McGaffin, Ken Lyons, Brian Chappell, Julie Joyce, Brian Gilley, and last but definitely not least, David Harry.

Foreword

by Mike Grehan

> "The world can be seen as only connections, nothing else . . ."
>
> —Sir Tim Berners Lee, inventor of the World Wide Web

For many, it's hard to imagine a time when Google didn't exist on the web. A time before we could simply type a few words into a box on a web page and magically be presented with all manner of content related to those keywords. Essentially, that's how most websites are found on the burgeoning World Wide Web, which continues to grow exponentially each and every day.

I launched my first online business in 1995, well before Google changed the web. My background is in media and marketing. I spent ten years in broadcast media followed by ten years in marketing on both the agency side and the client side. By 1995 I'd been aware of the web for some years and certainly recognized the potential from a commercial point of view. My partner in the business knew how to code HTML and build websites, most of which consisted of a few pages of text, a couple of jpg images, and a contact form.

The more websites we built, the better we got at it. But there was one vital, missing component to each of those sites, which rapidly became apparent to our customers: traffic.

Building websites wasn't the hard part of the job. Trying to figure out how to get visitors to them was. There's this famous quote, something along the lines of, "If you build it, they will come." It gets attributed to everybody from astronauts to movie characters. Regardless, whoever it was who said that was not a web developer or an online marketer. Because build we did, and come they didn't.

That same year, 1995, a guy by the name of Jeff Bezos had this remarkably dumb idea (I thought at the time) of launching a website to sell books. Books of all things. Jeez, Jeff, there's a bookstore on every corner in the city. I can pop in, buy one, and have the first chapter finished by the end of my lunch break. And you want me to give you my credit card details online and then wait up to five days before it hits my mailbox?

But more to the point, even if buying a book online was a good idea, how would Bezos get traffic? Like I say, back then, we all knew what the hard part was.

Enter Eric Ward.

Eric Ward started operating a website-awareness-building service in 1994. Today he provides a must-read linking strategies newsletter called *LinkMoses Private* (ericward. com/lmp), but back then one of his first tasks was to contact Jerry Yang (who at the time was a graduate student at Stanford and co-founder of Yahoo!) to point out that the directory didn't have a section for web promotion. And that's what Eric did via his newly formed NetPOST and URLwire services. This was not a press release distribution service that just randomly peppered the web with the usual digital dross. This was a private email list Eric ran, made up of subscribers who were genuinely interested in hearing about new stuff on the web (a kind of early-day alerts service). And what happened when he announced a new website? It attracted links!

How could Jeff Bezos resist?

Now, I'm not going to suggest for a second that Eric Ward is responsible for the success of Amazon in becoming the world's largest online retailer (although I will personally admit to being one of the world's largest nitwits for thinking it was a dumb idea in the first place). However, I will absolutely give credit to Eric Ward for being the father of what we now know as link-building services.

Soon, his sleeves were rolled up and he became master of the art of convincing people to link to Amazon and drive traffic. But not just Amazon, to the new customers he started acquiring on almost a daily basis. Imagine, this is a guy, in web-marketing terms, performing something akin to CPR.

However, Eric wasn't the only guy with the power of links on his mind. By 1998 Larry Page, co-founder of Google, had developed an algorithm largely based on social network analysis and network theory. Basically, Google was able to analyze the complex graph structure of the web and rank documents according to relativity based on the links that pointed to them.

It was the gold rush all over again. But this time the term for gold was *backlink*!

Once the online marketing community discovered the power of links in Google's ranking algorithm, the race to the top was on. A top-ten listing at Google for a competitive keyword or phrase can drive hundreds, even thousands of visitors (or more) to any given website.

The thing is, not all links are equal. Some are more equal than others. And some are infinitely more equal. Search engines apart, one link can send more traffic than another. You'll always have good and bad links. However, inside the Google algorithm, the quality of links vastly outweighs the quantity. And if you try to artificially inflate your "link popularity"—what Google giveth, Google can also, and surely does, taketh away!

I coined the term "black hat, white hat" sometime around 2002. It was based on something I noticed in cowboy movies when I was a kid. The good cowboys all wore white hats and the bad guys wore black. I used it as an analogy for those online marketers who stuck to Google's guidelines (particularly around linking practices) and those who didn't.

The industry has become fixated on getting links, but by any means possible. And that can be a very dangerous thing. Link building has now become a combination of understanding hugely complex ranking algorithms while applying the gentle art of persuasion.

Eric Ward and I have known each other for a very long time. We've shared the stage at many conferences discussing both the art and the science of developing a long-term, quality link-building strategy. And we both agree that if you frame this as just "getting links," then you'll probably fail in your efforts to dominate the search engine results pages (SERPs). Because the truth is, quality links are usually the byproduct of a good online marketing plan.

If you're a website owner, then no doubt your inbox has already been spammed with numerous emails from people who, as Eric puts it, offer to "link to your crap if you'll link to mine." Most likely you've had offers from foreign shores from companies offering to get you x number of links each week for $x per link.

It's likely that you've even dared to venture to reply to one of these emails to see how it works. But before you even seriously consider that and before you read the rare wisdom contained in this book, I want you to do one thing. I want you to go to your own website right now, take a pen and a piece of paper, and write down ten good reasons why you should link to your own website.

Now, if you find yourself scratching your head after four or five, ask yourself this question: If I can't think of ten good reasons to link to my website, what makes me think other people would?

Seriously, I've asked everyone from owners/managers of small businesses to CMOs of major international corporations the same question and seen the same head-scratching. It's hard to say the word *search* without adding the word *social* these days. Social media sites such as Facebook, LinkedIn, Twitter, and Google+ generate links by the millions as people connect, communicate, and share. The web has changed from a web of things to a web of people. And it's all about connections; about the way we're all linked together by one thing or another.

From content development and integrated marketing techniques to purely tactical link bait, you're about to learn directly from one of the masters of online marketing. In this book, the "Moses" of link building (as Eric is fondly known in the industry) will teach you how to wisely:

- Carry out a link audit and competitor analysis
- Develop a structured, long-term link-building strategy
- Identify and approach quality, top-ranking websites with a value proposition
- Differentiate links for traffic vs. links for ranking
- Recommend the tools of the trade for ethical link-building practices
- Keep on the right side of search engine guidelines
- Become slimmer and more attractive to the opposite sex and enlarge certain parts of your anatomy

Eric Ward is hands-down the smartest thinker in the space when it comes to link building. I guarantee this book will open up any mental blocks you've had about where to get started and set you on a path to becoming a link magnet.

Introduction
by Ken McGaffin

WHY I READ EVERYTHING GARRETT FRENCH WRITES ABOUT LINK BUILDING

I've been working with Garrett French on almost a weekly basis over the past 12 months. As you can imagine, we spend a lot of time talking about link building; and no matter what the finer points of the discussion, or what obscure aspect of the art we're talking about, I can be pretty sure that at some point Garrett will say something like, "I wonder if there's a tool to do that?" or "Hey, that would make a pretty good tool," or "How could we do that at scale?"

You see, Garrett French loves link-building tools.

He loves using them, he loves talking about them, and he loves creating them—and he has created some gems in his time.

That's good news for anyone who wants to learn about link building.

Why? Because Garrett's passion for creating tools is really a passion for solving link-building problems. And to create tools that solve link-building problems you need to have three attributes:

1. You've got to have a deep knowledge of all the processes of link building. Not just the big picture, but the nitty-gritty details of what actually needs to be done.

2. You've got to have the creative ability to take those processes and distill them into logical steps that make things easy for other people to understand and implement.

3. You've got to know how to do it all at scale—in a way that lets agencies and individuals zip through complex processes and say, "Well, that was easy, wasn't it?"

Garrett has all three essential attributes in spades. He's one of the most practical people I know working in this space: He talks and writes about link building with great passion, with great insight, and with a wonderful ability to communicate.

That's why I'm so excited by this collaboration with link-building legend Eric Ward.

Both these guys write stuff that, when it hits my inbox, makes me stop what I'm doing, make myself a brew of strong coffee, and sit down for a good read. I can't imagine a better pairing.

—Ken McGaffin
http://LinkingMatters.com

BONUS CONTENT!

A special password found in the book will grant you access to bonus content written and curated by the authors especially for buyers of the book. This content will include videos, tips, podcasts, and links to tools to help you continue on your quest to obtain the most powerful links possible for your site!

Go to www.ericward.com/book/

The password is

ultimatelinks

Chapter 1

A Brief Introduction to Search, Links, and Link Building

"A link is a connection from one web resource to another." This quote from the World Wide Web Consortium (W3C) makes web links sound so simple. And in some ways they are, or at least were intended to be. But the web as a whole is huge and complex, made up of trillions of individual pages, files, and other content, while at its core the web is simple, and made up of only two things: content and links.

Lots of links.

More links than any one person or search engine can count. Those links between pages and sites are the primary way web users navigate from one place to another online. A simple mouse click takes you from one site to another site, or from a search result to a specific page, or to a video, or a picture, or a song.

If you don't have a website, you probably haven't given much thought to links. But if you do have a website, be it a small blog or a huge corporate presence, then links take on a whole new meaning. In fact, links on the web will help determine the level of success your site will have on the web. In addition to the "humans" clicking on those links, every major "bot" (search engine) uses some form of link analysis when determining search results.

The purpose of this book is to simplify the complex online world of web links and help website owners create and execute link-building campaigns that attract links, increase traffic, and improve search rank.

A BRIEF HISTORY OF LINKS AND SEARCH ENGINES

In the beginning . . .

As much as we take the web for granted today, it was only a little more than 20 years ago that the very first website was created. No other websites linked to it because there were no other websites.

And there were no search engines to use to find it.

The world's first-ever website and web server, http://Info.cern.ch, launched on August 6, 1991, by the web's creator, Tim Berners-Lee, an engineer, computer scientist, and MIT professor (see Figure 1–1).

FIGURE 1–1. Info.cern.ch: The World's First-Ever Website

The site still exists today, and there are more than a half-million other websites that now link to it. A half-million links. That sounds like a lot of links, doesn't it?

Google.com also exists today (see Figure 1–2 on page 3). Hundreds of millions of sites link to Google.com, and more than 1 billion searches are performed there every day. Having your site appear high in a search engine's natural search results can be very

FIGURE 1–2. Google's Search Box

profitable for most businesses. However, very few people outside of Google and Bing really understand how search engines compile results, and even fewer understand how to affect those results, i.e., make a site rank higher.

There are many factors, and one of the most important of them is links from other sites to yours. The web of today is comprised of trillions of links between sites. Somehow, Google and other search engines analyze these links and draw conclusions about your site based on the links that point to your site.

Like a fingerprint, your links uniquely tell Google about your site. Who links to you and how they link to you is now one of the single most important factors that all search engines rely on when ranking results.

It didn't start out that way. The web's first search engine, called Wandex (see Figure 1–3), and the engines that followed (most of which are gone now), didn't analyze links at all. They only analyzed your website, the assumption being that your website would be the most accurate way to determine what your website was about.

As logical as that sounds, it didn't take long for web marketers to figure out how search engines worked, and could be manipulated, and the game was on.

FIGURE 1–3. The Web's First Search Engine, Called Wandex

As the years went by, search results became less and less accurate, with those most adept at manipulating the results being the big winners, while the searcher often ended up on a page that was not very helpful.

ENTER GOOGLE . . .

Then Google came along with the idea of using the very fabric of the web itself, links between sites, as a method for determining which web pages were most relevant for any given search.

In other words, the web would collectively determine where a site should rank, based on which sites attracted links. Think of a link as a vote. And while on the web, some votes matter more than others, and some can actually *hurt* your search rank, it's the best analogy to use to introduce you to the concept of link building.

Put simply, you can directly impact your search rankings if you understand how and why links matter and what you have to do in order to earn them. It isn't about quantity, it's about quality. A few links from the right places are better than a ton of links from sites with no value.

Link building is both art and science. There are many ways to build links. There's what some people call the "white-hat" approach, where you have a website devoted to a particular topic and you look for and contact people who care about that topic.

You let them know about your site in hopes that they'll link to your site from their site. This is a slow and methodical process, and it can produce amazing results if done correctly.

But there are other approaches, like sending a few million email messages to a list of people you don't know, with links in your email telling them about your site. This is commonly referred to as "spam."

The approach you choose for building links should be based on the content of your site, not spam. Automated link building does not result in your site earning quality links that will help your search rank.

For example, if you have an e-commerce site with generic products that can be purchased anywhere, why would anybody link to that site? There are 500 other sites where someone could buy the same product. For instance, take a look at the results for a search on "golf clubs" in Figure 1–4, page 5.

Why would another site link to your site instead of any of those other 500? The truth is, in this scenario, you'll have a hard time building links without paying for them. On the other hand, the more freely you create and provide unique content about subjects that you have some passion for, the more freely you will find your site able to attract and earn links. It's not as complicated as you think, really. My colleagues have

FIGURE 1-4. 146 Million Results for a Google Search on the Phrase "Golf Clubs"

often heard me say, "Every site has its own linking potential, depending on its subject matter, depth of content, and intended audience."

What I mean by this is the best target sites for your site to pursue and earn links from are going to be different from those for another site. Here's a great example. If you have a site that sells archery equipment and that also has excellent archery-related content, here's a target site, in Figure 1–5, you would want to have a link from. Prepare to be surprised.

Why is that site so valuable? Think of that site's intent, purpose, and author credibility. It's legitimate and trustworthy, and you can't get a link from this site just because you want one. You have to EARN it. You have to have archery-related content of

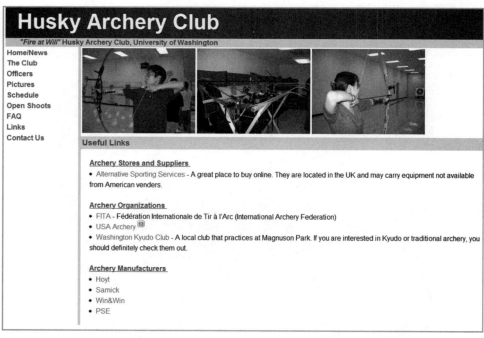

FIGURE 1-5. A Valuable Link for an Archery Products Online Retailer
http://students.washington.edu/archers/links.html

SeekBestSites.com

Website Directory

Home > Directory > Sports > Archery

[   ] [Search]

Archery

Sub-categories: None

This category doesn't contain any links

FIGURE 1–6. Sometimes Link Building is Knowing When NOT to Get the Link

merit. You have to find the owner/author of the site, you have to reach out to them in the proper way, and you have to recognize that not every site will be given a link, which is one additional reason the engines trust that site. Content of merit earns these types of links.

Now take a look at the site in Figure 1–6.

Which of the two sites do you feel was created by a group with a singular interest and passion for archery? The answer is obvious when you look at a pair of sites about a very specific topic, like those featured in Figures 1–5 and 1–6. Unfortunately, the overwhelming majority of SEO and link-building services you can buy today are not going to help you, could hurt you (penalties), and at best will be ignored as if they do not exist. You will have spent money for nothing.

FIGURE 1–7. What Makes a Site Worthy of a Link?

While outright penalties and banning from the engines are rare, and can be corrected over time, this is a slippery slope to be standing on while building links. It's also true that you often cannot control who links to you, so the engines must be cautious about levying a penalty until they have enough evidence. But here's a way you might want to think about it. Google employs hundreds of computer scientists and librarians, all of whom are a lot smarter than most of us are. They work every day to improve Google's ability to identify link spam, paid links, link networks, and other linking schemes. If we can spot link spam, it's only a matter of time before they will. Do you want to base your linking strategy on trying to fool a few hundred computer science Ph.D.s who are being paid to produce the most accurate search results possible?

Chapter 2

What Makes a Website Link-Worthy?

So what is the motivation for one website owner to link to another website?

The fundamental principle of the web is to allow any document to link to and to be linked from any other document. This is how Sir Tim Berners-Lee intended it when he first proposed the hypertext protocol in 1989 as a way to help researchers interlink related documents from computers all over the world.

It's interesting that nearly every commercially related web development since its founding has been in some way related to the link (that is, an attempt to find new ways for one site to be linked to another). Banner ads are, at their core, just a link from one site to another. So are text ads, whether on websites or in newsletters, or in an email message. And Like buttons, badges, icons, etc., are all just another form of link. A pay-per-click (PPC) listing or a Tweeted URL or a list of search results are nothing more than links. Your Yahoo! directory listing, BBB member page listing, even that cool widget you created—no matter how you spin it—are all links. Anything to be clicked on that shuttles people from one place to another while online constitutes a link.

The development of all forms and fashion of linking types has never improved on the original, and no amount of cleverness will ever change

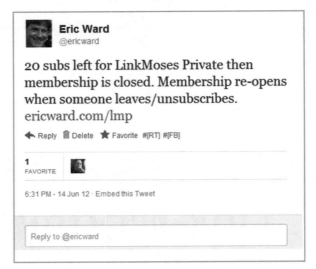

FIGURE 2–1. Even an Individual Tweet Can Contain a Link

one universal truth: The less useful your content, the less likely you are to ever receive a link to it. Let me write that again, and as you read it, try to sound like James Earl Jones:

The less useful your content,
The less likely you are to ever receive a link to it.

If we think of the word "useful" as a continuum, then the most useful sites are those that provide rich quality content on a specific subject on which the editor or provider is an authority. Think of the U.S. Government's National Cancer Institute (what was once known as CancerNet). Located at www.cancer.gov, the site is the ultimate example of content on the right side of the continuum—tens of thousands of pages on every facet of cancer, all free, all generated by experts in the field. See Figure 2–2 on page 11.

In fact, with no online marketing department, the National Cancer Institute's website has tens of thousands of links pointing to it from other sites around the world. It's one of my standard sermons: Useful content gets linked. When CancerNet hired me for some link analysis and strategy, there wasn't a whole lot for me to do. It took me less than a month to augment and improve what was already in place—a great collection of inbound links. My impact was minimal, if any.

But the reality is we can't all be the National Cancer Institute. Most sites simply do not have the kind of content that engenders tens of thousands of links. So what do you do? What if you are simply trying to sell a few widgets and don't have any reference to quality content? If your site lands on the left side of the useful continuum, you accept that you are not going to get many links. And those links you do get you will probably

FIGURE 2–2. National Cancer Institute's Homepage

have to pay for. And those links you pay for are not likely to help your rankings, and might even hurt them.

If you don't want to accept this reality and truly want to earn links to your site, you have one (and only one) other option available to you: Make it link-worthy.

What is a link-worthy site? Let's imagine you have an online magic store that caters to professional and amateur magicians. On your site, you sell tricks, supplies, hats, capes, and wands, even the saw-the-person-in-half gag.

If your content were nothing more than an online store, why would anyone link to it? You might get a few links on any magic-site web guides and link lists. But then what? If you are an online store with nothing but products as your content, then you MUST look to associate/affiliate programs as a means of generating links. Basically, you're paying for them.

But maybe there is something more you can do, if you are willing to roll up your sleeves.

What if, along with your products, you create a searchable database of information on magic? What if you had complete biographies of more than 700 magicians? What if you had a section devoted to magical world records, or a glossary of magical terms, or a directory of magicians on the internet?

FIGURE 2–3. MagicTricks.com Is a Great Example of an Ecommerce Site that Has Added Link-worthy Content

This would then be an excellent example of how a store site can add rich, relevant content, value, interest, and community to its website, as well as sell merchandise. Just about any writer who writes about magic and/or reviews websites would write about this site, and any magic fan with a website and a curated list of handpicked links would be likely to link to it.

The above is not just a wide-eyed, hypothetical example. It exists at http://www. MagicTricks.com, featured in Figure 2–3.

I know from experience it's difficult to find high-trust online venues and curator/ site reviewers willing to link to sales sites. The more a site offers deep information on a certain subject in the form of databases, community, guides, forums, reviews, etc., the more likely editors or curators will feature it in their own content. Whether it's a business or consumer site, the content-richer the better, especially if the site's mission is sales. A site designed to sell a product is far different from a true reference site with hundreds and hundreds of pages of free information on a particular subject.

The National Cancer Institute and MagicTricks.com could not be more different from each other, yet they do have one incredibly important thing in common: Both have topic-specific content written by passionate experts.

The best analogy I can think of to explain a sales-focused website is a public library. A library is, first and foremost, about content, although it does sell things. You can buy copies of books, order maps, buy online database search time, or rent study offices or PCs. Some libraries even have video-rental services and snack shops or restaurants. Money definitely changes hands at a library. But nobody would confuse this commerce with a library's true mission: being content curators and helping patrons find that content.

In like manner, a website also needs to be a library of information on whatever its focus might be. Add great content to your product site.

Why bother?

Because useful content gets linked. Products don't.

FIGURE 2–4. The More You Can Make Your Site Like a Library of Content, the More Likely You Are to Attract Links to It

Chapter 3

Link-Building Campaign Design

Quite often, link builders working outside of your organization will design campaigns based on their personal or agency strengths, tools, and processes. When the campaign ends, the links stop.

For example, in our work with clients, which typically involves expert engagement (often bloggers or other publishing experts in a space), much of the value we create is in the relationships established, not to mention the expert content we create.

When we stop engaging the experts, the relationships cool back off and the link momentum slows down. This is because our clients have typically not developed the infrastructure and processes to keep developing these relationships (this book is for them). For link-building agencies specializing in link buys or rentals, the decline in momentum can be even more drastic.

Designing an effective, sustainable link-building campaign (or series of campaigns) requires a delicate balance and a precise understanding of an organization's strengths and weaknesses, as well as carefully described and easy-to-measure goals. This chapter will help you to more effectively design and measure your next link-building campaign. At the very least, it will get you thinking a bit more broadly about link building!

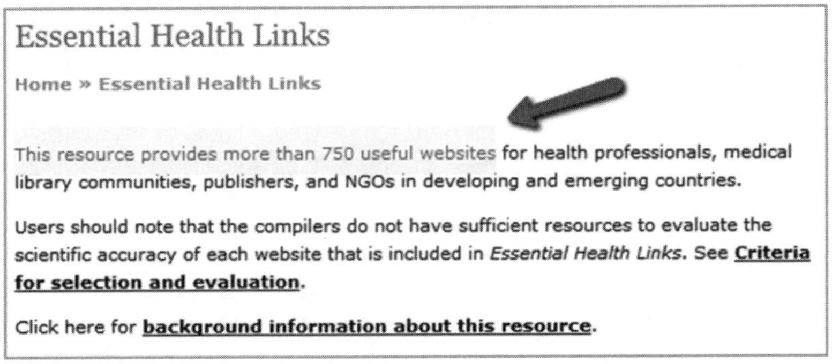

FIGURE 3–1. Knowing How to Find the Expert Link "Curators" Is Always Useful

PLANNING CAMPAIGN SCOPE: SIX FACTORS THAT IMPACT CAMPAIGN DESIGN

There are six broad factors we've discovered that impact a link-building campaign's scope. Ideally a link builder in the campaign design phase has a suitable amount of time to think about and consider all these factors. In doing so, he will probably discover a few more factors unique to his organization's situation. This is great—the more factors you can take into consideration and design for, the more unique and effective your campaign will be.

Factor 1: What's Working Well for You Already?

We like to start client discussions with a question about what's working well already. And not just in link building! For example, on a recent prospect call, we asked how they currently generated their leads. It turned out they had an email list of 10,000 subscribers that they'd built up a great relationship with over the course of the past 10 to 15 years! They estimated that at least 10 percent of their list comprised active web content publishers, which made this list the perfect place to begin designing a campaign.

On the more link-oriented side, we ran through some questions with a prospect recently to discover their linkable assets. They didn't have time or resources to create content, which is our organization's linkable asset strength. When we asked what had been working, they mentioned that they had products that they could give away for nonprofits and bloggers to use as prizes in raffles and other types of contests. This understanding then informed the link opportunities we discovered for them in that we were able to systematically discover massive numbers of prequalified prospects.

We encourage organizations to think about what's working well already, and to keep that in mind throughout all the discussion in this book. Supporting and growing from what works can be far easier and more economical than trying to create something entirely new that does not stem from currently existing strengths.

Factor 2: Your Business and Marketing Goals

Specific business and marketing goals are often missing in link-building campaign design, especially when a campaign is designed in a vacuum without input from other departments.

Because link building has the capacity to impact goals far beyond your SERP (search engine results page) rankings, we highly recommend that link builders understand and support the company's specific business and marketing goals in the campaign design phase. Not only will this ensure the link builders have a continued role in the organization, but by solving the problem of "how can link building support x," they will uncover a solution that may be unique in the market. The link-building goals section starting on page 21 demonstrates some things link building can impact, but it's far more important to start with your organization's goals in mind!

Factor 3: Your Linkable Assets

What about your organization is linkable? This includes people, your organization's brand, your organization's story, your free tools or widgets, your unique and helpful

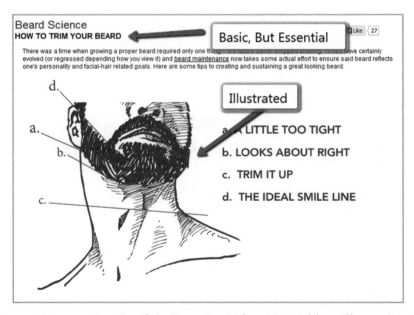

FIGURE 3–2. Content Can Be Plain Text, But When You Add an Illustration to That Text, It Becomes Potentially More "Linkable"

content, your available resources, and more. Further, consider that your industry's definition of "linkable" can and will differ from those of other industries. If all your competitors have free web tools, then this is no longer a strong differentiator and may not incite interest and links.

See Chapter 5 for an overview of Linkable Assets, from discovering them on your site and within your organization to identifying what your competitors and industry publishers have done to attract links.

Factor 4: Link Opportunities in Your Space

The link opportunities that exist from market to market can be quite different. For example, if you're targeting a consumer market, it could be that work-at-home-dad bloggers are a key segment for you. If you sell specialty bulldozer parts, then engaging the daddy bloggers might not make as much sense.

Your market—in particular, the publishers catering to your market that you want to earn links from—determines the scope and type of opportunities available to you.

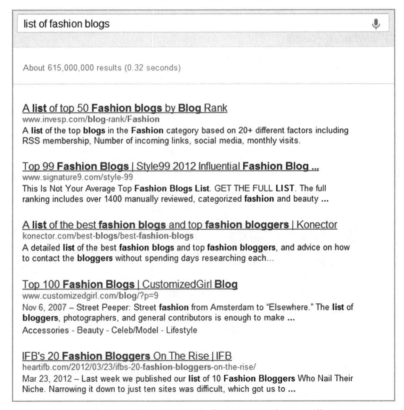

FIGURE 3–3. Remember to Always Look for Lists—They Will Save You Hours of Searching. Further, the Presence of Lists Indicates a Robust Publishing Niche.

Factor 5: Departments Requiring Input Plus Your Influence Within the Organization

We've found sometimes that, when operating as a link-building agency, we're working with the search engine optimization (SEO) department within an organization. Our methods typically involve content creation and industry expert engagement. This sometimes means we have to get sign-off from departments like PR, content strategy, social media, marketing, even the CEO before the campaign can really get rolling.

We typically try to identify the department that our contact is most embedded within, the department in which they have the most influence. And then we work to keep the campaign within their authority so that we can have the fastest impact. The more departments requiring input, the more work the link builder will have to do in mediating cross-departmental concerns.

However, for sustainable, ongoing link-building campaigns (and often these may NOT be called link-building campaigns internally), you will need to work the political scene within your organization and be constantly on the lookout for ways to "link-enhance" what others are already doing.

Factor 6: Your Available Resources

At the end of the day, your link-building campaign will come down to the amount of time and money you can put into it. Knowing how much time you can spend yourself, and how much work you can ask for or require of others, can help you to define the entire scope of the project. Often—and rightfully so—your available resources hinge on your abilities as a link builder, as well as your abilities in effectively communicating probable and actual returns on investment. In Chapter 4 we will look at some probable areas of link building's return.

Toward Effective Link-Building Campaign Metrics

While "get more links" may be what your boss or your clients or even your SEO recommends, how and why you get these links pointed at your pages will impact the long-term viability of your links as well as the value they pass along to your site. Before designing your campaign, we believe it's important to have a general sense of what you can effect with your work as a link builder.

Traditionally, link builders have sought search engine impact and measured their success based on increases in the SERPs. Increasingly though, link builders have begun looking for metrics beyond SERP influence. This chapter looks at goals and areas of influence in both categories.

LINK BUILDING AS SEARCH ENGINE IMPACT

Search engine algorithms use links to make decisions about your site as a whole, and its pages in particular. The classic way of describing a link's value—as search engines perceive it—is that it is a "vote" for the page it's pointing to. The link out suggests that this other page is relevant and worth investigating, just as the citations in an academic journal point you toward original sources of thought, concept, or data that support the discussion.

Increase Perceived Trust/Authority of Your Site

You will see an increase in organic traffic after receiving links from sites that have already earned trust and proven their authority to search engines. These kinds of links help across the board for terms you're targeting, and benefit sites best if the sites are already well optimized and without major issues. You'll have little to no ability to guide the keyword impact of these kinds of links (unless you're buying the links, or you've developed clever campaigns).

Adjust Perceived Relevance of Your Site

Links can and do send signals to search engines regarding what your site is about, what industries and markets it serves, and the keyword clusters it's most related to. If you're expanding your market focus, or if you're just getting started, links that help connect you to "market spaces" will help you immensely. You can think about relevance in terms of your geographical location as well, and links and other types of citations can help indicate to search engines that you can and should appear in the SERPs targeting specific geo-locations.

Direct SERP Keyword Impact Through Anchor Text Manipulation

The classic role of link builders has been, through buying or placing links with specific keywords in the anchor text, to directly impact their site's rankings for those keywords. This is still effective, and often described as the most effective way to secure rankings. It's probable that search engines will evolve past anchor text as a key factor in SERP rankings, however.

What to Measure for Link Building for Search Engine Impact

If affecting search results is your core focus for link building, here are a number of things you can work on influencing:

- Search rankings for converting key terms
- Percentage of increase in converting search traffic
- Percentage of increase in search traffic from geographic regions
- Increase in number of pages on domain that yield traffic
- Percentage increase in non-branded search traffic
- Percentage fluctuation in engagement metrics such as time on site, time on pages, and bounce rate
- Number plus location of links from sites/people deemed authoritative
- Number plus location of links from sites/people deemed relevant

LINK BUILDING AS MARKET ENGAGEMENT

In addition to impacting search results, links can and do powerfully impact how the market perceives your business. The benefits beyond search are often obscured in SEO-oriented link-building discussions, and often these areas of impact are beyond a typical SEO department's authority within an organization. If you're an SEO seeking to drive more links in your organization, it will make sense to learn more about this kind of thinking and be ready and able to discuss it with the appropriate people internally.

Build Company and Personal Brand

When your link-building efforts include expert engagement as well as content placement, you have an impact on how your market perceives you and your brand. This is especially true if you've done your research and know which publications in your market exert the most influence on your business prospects.

Earning mentions—on a monthly basis—in the top publications in your market keeps your brand relevant. If you've designed your campaign carefully, or if you've worked closely with PR and communicated your SEO needs effectively, you can often get great keywords in your anchor text.

SERP impact is just a side benefit here though; it's more about your perceived importance and value in the market!

FIGURE 4–1. Aaron Wall of SEObook Is a Great Example of a
Personal Brand on the Web

Build Your Lead Pipeline

We've found that the links we've earned as a byproduct of building our brand (with interviews and placed how-to content) also generate business leads. In fact, long before we saw search traffic, we saw relevant referral traffic that turned into sales. From an SEO perspective, the links we've earned in this manner are all highly relevant, and many of them are from high-authority sites in the SEO/SEM space. From a bottom-line perspective, these links have been the lifeblood of our growing company.

Engage the Expert Community and Guide Conversation

We advocate expert interviews and surveys as a cornerstone of content designed to attract links. If you engage your industry's experts carefully and intelligently, you'll see that you can begin guiding market conversations. Guiding conversations doesn't mean being manipulative; it means pushing conversation forward in a way that benefits the market, as well as your organization. The benefit of expert engagement is that the experts are likely to link to content created through that engagement, as well as be more open to your requests to link to or mention your content in the future.

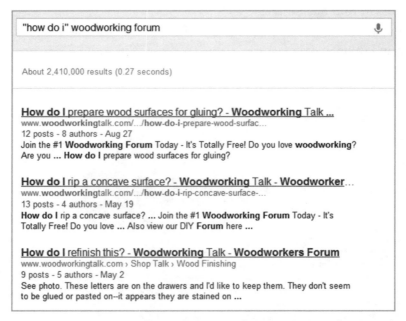

FIGURE 4–2. You Can Usually Find a Topical Forum in Nearly any Subject, Where Experts Are Discussing that Subject

What to Measure in Link Building for Market Impact

Here are some suggestions for data points you can measure when demonstrating link building's impact beyond the SERPs. We hope that these help you to formulate your own metrics, and that they help you to powerfully demonstrate the value of links to other departments in your organization.

- Percentage increase in targeted referral traffic
- Percentage increase in referral traffic conversions
- Percentage increase in engagement metrics such as time on site, time on pages, and decrease in bounce rate
- Percentage increase in branded search term traffic
- Percentage increase of mentions in target media over competitors
- Number of blog posts and articles about or citing your organization
- Number of customers indicating that media provoked their inquiry
- Number of third-party mentions and community pass-alongs
- Number of positive responses in conversation thread exchanges
- Number of key influencers known to actively suggest your products or services to those who trust them
- Number of positive, goal-focused emails exchanged
- Number of newsletter/RSS subscriptions increase

Chapter 5

Linkable Assets

Linkable assets are the experts, pages, widgets, tools, discounts, relationships and any other people or pages related to your organization that incentivize others to share a link with their site visitors. When analyzing competitor backlinks for link prospects, it's often difficult to determine next steps because your competitors have different linkable assets from yours.

When you understand what's linkable about your organization, as well as what types of assets earn links in your market, you will have a much easier time identifying your link opportunity types. Knowing these types makes you more effective at prospecting for these opportunities.

LINKABLE ASSET ANALYSIS

Linkable asset analysis is the process of systematically analyzing your site and your competitors' sites, as well as noncompeting publishers' sites in your keyword space, to identify what typically earns links and what *could* earn links but doesn't already. If yours is an especially large site or organization, this process can and should take some time.

COMMON LINKABLE ASSET CATEGORIES

These linkable asset categories will help get you thinking about what your organization's linkable assets could be. Thinking broadly and creatively at the beginning of a link-building campaign or project engagement can open you up to a stronger, more effective campaign design. After all, you could be sitting on a link magnet and not even realize it!

Free Apps and Tools on Your Site

Do you provide any free applications or web-based tools to your site visitors? If so, it's likely that these have already attracted links naturally. If you haven't promoted these tools yet for the purpose of link building, then these assets could help you to develop even more links. Be careful though when designing and building a tool or app—they can be expensive (sometimes two to three times what you expect, or what you're quoted), can seem to take forever to develop, and could still flop. That said, nothing demonstrates your expertise like a custom tool you've crafted to make your customers' lives easier. One such tool is BuzzStream.

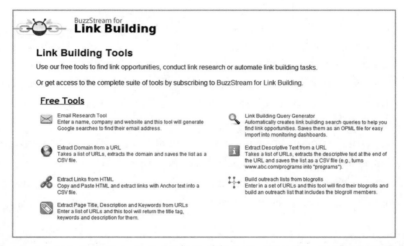

FIGURE 5–1. BuzzStream's Link-Building Process Management Tool

Products/Services to Give Away for Donations/Contests/Review

If you have products or services you can give away, you can earn links through donation thank-you pages, through contests, and via product/service reviews from experts in your market. Oftentimes this asset is one of the easiest paths to developing links. However, it's fairly easy for your competitors to emulate. Further, these approaches to link building can create enormous and unexpected logistical nightmares, such as shipping and packaging, or even getting the winner's contact information from the site conducting the giveaway.

Widgets, Tools, Images, Data for Publishers (Offsite)

Have you created widgets, tools, images, or data that publishers of other websites are free to add to their websites? Infographics, embeddable tools, research data, and other types of information created for the express purpose of giving it away is a classic and powerful method for earning links. If you have any of these assets and you haven't aggressively and extensively promoted them, then you're leaving valuable links and relationships on the table.

Thought Leaders and Subject Matter Experts

Are there thought leaders and subject matter experts in your organization? Do they have time to write or in some other way share their expertise with the market? These linkable assets could generate links in the form of interviews, guest posts, and quote contributions to industry news publications. If you have a PR or Social Media department, link builders should help them to identify link opportunities that these assets enable.

Partner Relationships

Do you have business partners, vendors, customers, and technology licensees? Each of these represents a potential link in the form of testimonials, published client lists, and "powered-by" buttons. Gather a list of your vendors and partners and look for ways to acquire (and give) links to all of them. Think interviews, think link requests for *their* vendors and partners pages, and think updated "powered-by" badges.

Job Listings, Events, and Coupons

If your organization consistently publishes job openings, puts on events, or launches new products, then you've got quite a few link opportunities open to you. Colleges and industry vertical sites are sometimes willing to link to pages that feature new job openings. Many cities have event calendars that will publish details about your event and post links on their site for sign-up and more information. If you consistently offer coupons to your customers, then you'll find massive numbers of coupon-listing sites, many of which link back. It's likely (though we haven't confirmed this) that there are niche and geo-targeted coupon sites. Niche and geo sites are confirmed to often exist for jobs and events.

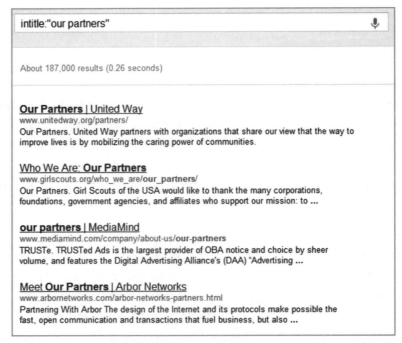

FIGURE 5–2. Google Search Result Shows Evidence of Websites Having "Partners"

FIGURE 5–3. Many Company Websites Have Pages Describing the Advantages of Working at That Company

Consistent Publishing via Blog, Video, Podcast, PDFs, Twitter, Etc.

Do you or does your organization publish content consistently? These linkable assets open you up to numerous link opportunity types from around your industry; everything from blog directories, to niche social news sites, to blog lists, to PDF submissions, and to distribution sites. In some industries the fact that your CEO blogs is link-worthy and notable in itself.

Budget

Money is almost always a linkable asset, in that if you have the money, you can offer it to another site in exchange for a link. However, the link opportunities that you can purchase are often easy for competitors to duplicate. Further, some search engines aggressively penalize (in the form of lowered search rankings) purchased links that aren't labeled or coded as advertisements, making them a potentially risky investment that could end up costing far more in damages than they bring in search traffic. Some sites, such as directories, require a budget as well.

IDENTIFYING COMPETITOR AND OTHER MARKET-DETERMINED LINKABLE ASSETS

It's also valuable to conduct linkable asset analysis on your competitors' sites and organizations, as well as on the sites of your industry's major news and information publishers. You can do this by running through the linkable asset category types above and determining which ones your competitors have. Here are several more ways to identify the linkable assets in your market.

How Do You Figure Out What Gets Links?

If you know your primary competitors, as well as the top publishers in your market, then you can use a variety of free and fee-based tools to identify the pages on their sites that have attracted the most links. These pages will help you get an idea of what your industry thinks of as "linkable." Paste the URLs of your competitors and top publishers into:

- LinkInsight from AdGooroo
- Ahrefs.com
- MajesticSEO.com
- Open Site Explorer

Each of these will help you identify the most-linked pages on sites that compete with you in the SERPs. These most-linked pages can help you to find the linkable asset in your space that could be the most beneficial to your campaign—or the asset that's been done to death!

What Gets Tweeted?

When you know your competitors and top publishers in your market, you can begin looking for what content gets mentioned frequently on Twitter. While we have not done studies to determine the correlation (if any) between links and tweets, it does stand that a tweet or other social mention is a citation that confers value. By extension, we can reasonably assume that what a market values enough to tweet, it values enough to link to (so long as there are expert publishers who publish outside of Twitter). We use http://search.twitter.com/. Search for your competition here and get an idea of what content of theirs gets published consistently on Twitter.

A PROCESS FOR IDENTIFYING AND EVALUATING YOUR EXISTING LINKABLE ASSETS

Your current linkable assets either exist on a page of your website—your blog, for example—or are located on someone else's website, such as an interview with your CEO that appears on an industry trade site.

Inventory Your Onsite Assets

One of the best ways to identify your existing linkable assets is with a thorough, section-by-section review of your site. This should include not only a by-hand visit to the major sections and important pages of your site, but a review of your site using Open Site Explorer, Majestic SEO, and Ahrefs.com. You need to identify what has attracted links already so that you can earn more links for your site, as well as what is linkable but hasn't earned links yet, so that you can introduce it to the corresponding link opportunities in your market.

Inventory Your Offsite Assets

Identifying offsite assets can be a bit trickier, often because you don't think of them as potentially linkable. Offsite assets include:

- Thought leaders within your organization
- Your PR department
- The web development team
- And more

Running through our list of link asset categories above could also spark some ideas, and competitor backlink analysis can also suggest some offsite assets in your organization that you haven't yet tapped into. Furthermore, your offsite assets typically will require some work on the part of others within your organization, which will require you to build a case for their involvement.

Links generated through engaging these wonderful people in your organization will often be of higher quality. The value of identifying your linkable assets prior to a link-building campaign is that you can assess what types of sites and opportunities these assets open up for you. For example, if your organization puts on teaching or training events around the country, then the events themselves are linkable assets. Knowing your linkable assets makes it much easier to identify the link opportunity types, as discussed in Chapter 6, which you'll need in order to conduct effective link acquisition with high rates of return.

Link Opportunity Types

Link opportunity types are the kinds of websites and specific pages of websites that are likely homes for links to your assets. Link opportunity types can include sites that accept guest posts and comments—that is, sites that actively seek and publish content from others. One of the oldest and most frequently mentioned link opportunity types is a directory, which is typically in the business of linking to websites.

The value of brainstorming your link opportunity types ahead of time is that you'll be able to build out more accurate and descriptive link-building queries, as well as qualify link prospects more quickly once you have them. Further, certain link opportunity types will need to be handled differently and by different people in your organization. Your CEO won't necessarily be the person to submit sites to niche directories, nor will your marketing intern be the right person to be interviewed by a prominent blogger. Knowing your link opportunity types will help you when designing your overall link-building campaign process.

GOING FROM LINKABLE ASSETS TO LINK OPPORTUNITY TYPES

In Chapter 5, we discussed linkable assets—the people and web pages associated with your organization that can attract links. You identify these assets for the purpose of identifying their associated opportunity types. Be aware though, it's possible—and sometimes vital—to go from link opportunity types back to developing linkable assets. Stay alert throughout your asset inventory and prospecting to new ideas and obvious opportunities.

Brainstorm Opportunity Types for Each Asset on Your List

Brainstorming opportunity types does take a bit of practice and experience, but as the link builder (and the SEO?) you're the best person suited for this job because you're the most familiar with the kinds of linking sites in your keyword space.

Let's walk through opportunity-type brainstorming for your CEO who has agreed to help out with link building in every way possible. He's been incredibly accommodating, and agreed to write two articles for placement and one article for the company blog as well as to participate in any interviews you can dig up for him. Further, he agreed to comment once a week on three notable articles at high-profile sites.

Your linkable asset in this scenario is a "thought leader." Your opportunity types include:

- Guest post and other content placement opportunities
- Blogs in your space that write roundups
- Industry news sites (assuming his company blog post is suitably noteworthy)
- Sites that have written interviews with other industry leaders
- Industry blogs that allow comments

Knowing and listing the opportunities you're looking for will help you when it comes time to develop your link-prospecting queries.

Here's another quick brainstorm, this time for a company that sells a specialized grooming brush for dogs with curly hair. In this organization, the CEO is distanced from the web side of the business, as he's always been a direct-mail believer. It's just the SEO doing link building, and with relatively little support. Our intrepid SEO has one highly linkable asset readily at his disposal—free doggie brushes he can send out. He's also got a video camera and a dog with curly hair so he can make some basic how-to videos.

This SEO's assets include the product itself, of which he has 50 he can send out. He also has five how-to videos for grooming dogs with curly hair. The opportunities he's looking for include:

- Pet-related charities that have thank-you pages for in-kind donors
- Doggy info and community bloggers who review products
- Dog info sites that feature videos

- Any bloggers who might be interested in using one of the doggy brushes as a prize in a contest

Primarily he's looking for nonprofits in the pet space and dog bloggers—it will be quite easy now to create link-prospecting queries. If he could squeeze in more time every week it might make sense to participate in a few forums relating to dog grooming, as well.

COMMON LINK OPPORTUNITY TYPES

Now that we've gone over a couple of sample brainstorms for going from linkable assets to link opportunities we'll look at some of the more common link opportunity types we've encountered in our work.

Content Placement Opportunities

Content placement opportunities include guest posts on industry blogs, op-ed pieces on industry news sites, how-tos placed in your industry's association newsletter, even RSS syndication (republishing your blog, basically) on select sites with targeted, relevant traffic. Content placement opportunities require content, which requires writers—ideally great writers who get your industry and know your subject well.

Company Profile Listings

Company profile listings occur typically on aggregation sites that publish job listings, company stock information, PDFs, coupons, events (including sales-oriented webinars), free web tools (including spreadsheets), free downloadable software, and more (we're constantly discovering new aggregation sites, and different industries have different aggregated content types). Some sites charge for publishing your information, and some don't. Some sites follow links to your site and some add the no-follow tag. Some sites link to you from every page on their site that mentions you, and some only link to you from your actual profile page. If you consistently have job openings, events, new PDFs, etc., then you should definitely investigate this opportunity type. Figure 6–1 on page 38 shows an example Company Profile link on popular couponing website RetailMeNot.com

Open Conversation Opportunities

Open conversation opportunities include things like:

- Blog comments

FIGURE 6–1. An Example of a Company Profile Page on the Popular Coupon Site RetailMeNot.com

- Forum discussions
- Question and answer sites
- Industry social networking sites

These are places where you can register, sometimes even create a profile, and then begin interacting with the community in ways that add value. If you have already created tools and information of value on your site, you can and should then proceed to direct folks that way via links. Please don't join just to link-drop though—only join the conversation on sites where you can genuinely become "a regular." The asset required here is subject matter expertise and time. Figure 6-2 on page 39 shows an online auto repair forum.

Editorial Mentions

Editorial mentions are links that occur in the body of an article. We're referring here to links that are earned either through merit or persistence, rather than earned through

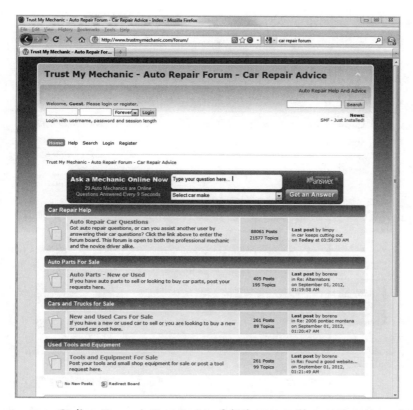

FIGURE 6–2. Online Forums Can Be Useful Places to Share Your Knowledge and Links to Your Assets

monetary payment. These can occur in reviews at industry news sites, direct content citations from other how-to writers, discussions of your company's news or blog statements, and even in content you place (see "Content Placement Opportunities" above). These types of links will all be hard earned through relationships you develop with the industry expert publishers in your market space.

Figure 6–3 on page 40 shows an example of an editorial mention.

Directory Listings

Similar to company profile listings, directory listings are common opportunities across industries. Debra Mastaler, a link-building industry authority on web directories and publisher of the blog LinkSpiel, says, "Ideally you're sourcing niche directories with high-touch editorial curation. The harder—even more expensive—it is to get listed, the better (usually). The beauty of directories is that typically they're relatively easy to acquire—just add your company's information. That low barrier of entry is also the problem with

FIGURE 6–3. When a Site Includes a Link to You within Their Editorial Content,
It Is Considered a Trustworthy Link

directories. However, there's no reason to turn up your nose at them. If you can find a few decent industry or geo-relevant directories, you should, by all means, acquire those links." Mastaler's LinkSpiel homepage is featured in Figure 6–4 on page 41.

Resource Lists

Resource lists come in many forms. Sometimes they're on library websites, and sometimes tucked away on long-forgotten university web pages. Sometimes they're in the form of massive resource aggregation sites (almost directories), and sometimes they get published on a weekly basis in the form of a roundup. If you have created—and continue to create—expert resources for your industry, then you should pursue this opportunity type.

See Figure 6–5 on page 42 for an example of a resource list for health.

FIGURE 6–4. Debra Mastaler Often Provides Excellent Advice about Web Directories on Her Blog at LinkSpiel.com

Sponsored Links

We have not sought experience in purchasing links. It is our understanding that the best purchased links are those that are difficult for search engines and competitors to detect, and that come in the body of highly relevant and high-quality content. Avoid sites that mention or discuss SEO, and definitely don't buy links on sites that advertise the sale of links (unless they are no-following and you're buying for traffic and exposure, not SERP impact). This type of opportunity, displayed in Figure 6–6, page 42, requires money.

FIGURE 6–5. Often Overlooked by Link Builders, Many Public Libraries Offer Topical Link Resource Lists. These Can Be Very Useful Links to Obtain.

FIGURE 6–6. Sponsoring Events or Organizations Can Earn You the Appreciation of Your Market, Spread Your Brand, and Drive Direct Traffic

Chapter 7

How to Conduct a Link Opportunity Analysis for Your Keyword Space

Knowing what link opportunities exist for a given market as defined by its keyword space can go a long way toward helping you design a link-building campaign. However, if you don't have the available resources to create new assets, then it may not do you much good to know about these opportunities. On the other hand, if you can clearly demonstrate link opportunities are available, this could open up new resources for you in your organization. This chapter provides some thinking and process suggestions for link builders trying to understand or "inventory" all the link opportunities for their market.

KNOW YOUR MARKET-DEFINING KEYWORDS (MDKWS)

Market-defining keywords are the keywords you'll be using throughout your link prospecting and market research. They are the "big head" keywords in your industry that would bring lots of traffic but few sales. Here are a few simple guidelines for determining your MDKWs.

Seven Characteristics of Market-Defining Keywords

1. Probably not converting keywords

2. Words the market or participants use to describe itself/themselves
3. Single or two-word phrases that are very crowded and competitive in the SERPs (not many ads targeting them)
4. Keywords you would not typically target with a pay-per-click (PPC) campaign
5. A root extracted from your PPC/SEO keywords
6. Common names for the practitioners within your industry (what are the experts actually called?)
7. Words commonly used in the names of publications within your market

Because this process requires actual queries in your search engine of choice, it's vital that you've identified your most productive, least "noisy" keywords that will help you really measure and gauge your market space.

DESIGN QUERIES FOR EACH OPPORTUNITY TYPE

Once you know your MDKWs, it's time to create queries and search them in your favorite search engine.

Look for Blogs, News Sites, and Trade Publications

The existence of blogs, news sites, and trade publications (such as Search Engine Watch and Search Engine Land) are all indicators of a healthy "expert publication" stratus within your market space. If these kinds of sites exist, especially in large numbers, your campaign design can and should include expert engagement and content creation and promotion, to name a couple. In Figure 7–1, page 45, we show the results of a search on dog blogs. Notice how huge the *dog* MDKW space is: 476 million results!

Check for these kinds of publishers with queries such as:

- MDKW blogs
- MDKW "blog list"
- "top MDKW blogs"
- "MDKW news"
- MDKW "Trade Publication"
- MDKW conference or convention (you will have to track back to the trade organization putting on the convention)

How many results in the top ten are relevant? Are you finding lists of bloggers? If not, make sure your MDKWs are broad enough! If so, then make note of "expert engagement" and content creation/promotion as a solid direction for your link-building efforts.

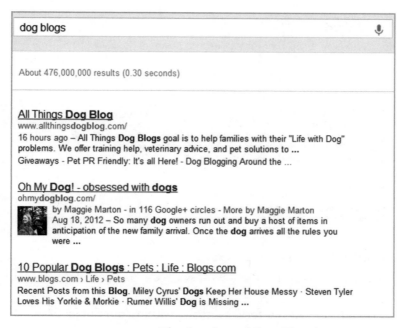

FIGURE 7–1. That's a Lot of Dog Blogs!

Look for Niche Directories

Niche directories are almost always worth submitting to. Consider them a "covering your bases" link-building effort. Some keyword spaces have niche directories and some don't. Figure 7–2 on page 46 features search results for dog directories, and Figure 7–3 on page 46 shows a niche directory for all things Elvis Presley.

Find niche directories with queries such as:

- "MDKW Directory"
- "MDKW Websites"
- MDKW "suggest * URL"

Look for Interviews with Subject Matter Experts

The presence of interviews signifies that there's an "expert class" within your keyword space. Figure 7–4 on page 47 demonstrates how to search for these. If there are a number of interviews then you should do two things. The first is to get thought-leaders in your organization interviewed. Second, you should conduct a group interview of all the experts who have received interviews. Gather the experts' contact information, come up

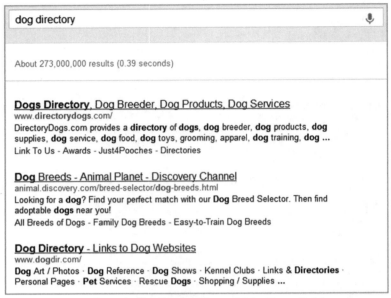

FIGURE 7–2. Search for Directories within Your Subject Area

FIGURE 7–3. There Are Directories for Just about Any Niche, Even a Directory Just for Sites about Elvis Presley

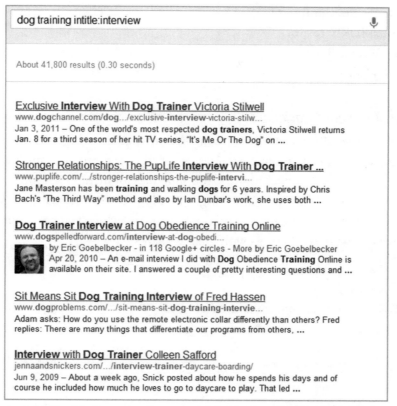

FIGURE 7–4. Add "Intitle:interview" to the MDKW for Which You're Seeking Experts. Here We Are Looking for Interviews with Expert Dog Trainers.

with between five and ten great questions and send them out. When they have responded, aggregate their answers into one article and let them know when it's published.

Check on the presence of interviews with queries such as:

- MDKW intitle:interview
- MDKW intitle:"q&a with"
- MDKW intitle:"tips from" OR "advice from" OR "chat with"

Look for Niche Forums, Social Networking Sites, and Q/A Sites

What is the online community like in your keyword space? Remember, not everyone has caught up with Web 2.0, and there are hundreds of thousands of people perfectly happy with forums as their platform for web interactions. Find them! This will help you to determine whether it's worthwhile to put resources into online conversations.

Find niche forums and social networks with queries such as:

- MDKW community
- intitle:MDKW forum
- MDKW inurl:blogs
- MDKW answers

Look for Professional Associations

Professional associations indicate a high level of business organization within an industry. Figure 7–5 below shows us the results of a query for dog-training associations. This means some great opportunities for link development. First off, you should consider joining as a means of connecting formally with your industry. Second, many associations have online newsletters and publications to which you can submit content.

Find professional associations with queries such as:

- MDKW association
- MDKW associated
- MDKW intitle:"of america" (or other locale)

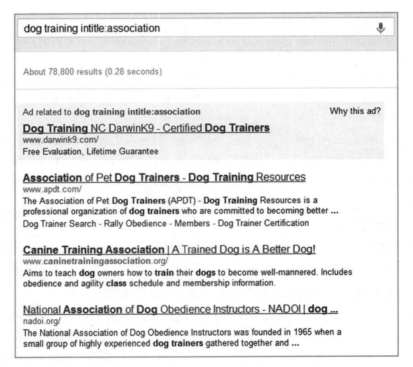

FIGURE 7–5. The "Intitle:association" Command with "Dog Training" Gives Us Search Results for Dog-Training Associations on the Internet

Look for Company Profile Listing Opportunities

Company profile listings—often earned through submitting specific content types to aggregation sites—are a fairly simple and easy way to build links. There are usually paid and unpaid opportunities. See Figure 7–6.

FIGURE 7–6. Eric Ward's Company Profile as Shown in SEOmoz's Recommended Companies Listing at www.seomoz.org/article/recommended

Find company profile listing opportunities with queries like:

- MDKW add job*
- MDKW submit software
- MDKW submit pdf
- MDKW add coupon
- MDKW submit contest
- MDKW events
- MDKW free tools

Look for Resource Curators

Resource curation has until recently been the task of librarians. These days it's far more likely that industry expert participants and publishers will build out lists of resources either on a one-time basis with continual updates (that is what we mean by "curation"), or on a weekly/monthly basis in the form of roundups. We've seen some resource aggregation in the form of exhaustive how-tos that link out to the best industry tools and information as well, so be on the lookout!

Detect resource curators with queries such as:

- MDKW roundup
- "Useful MDKW links" library
- MDKW resources list

Look for Content Placement Opportunities

Guest content placement has been the work of the PR department for years. Times are changing, and it's up to link builders to help lead the company toward content placements that will improve rankings, sales, and brand recognition.

Check your keyword space for content placement opportunities with queries such as:

- MDKW "guest post"
- MDKW inurl:category/guest
- MDKW "guest article"
- MDKW "write for us"

ANALYZING YOUR RESULTS AND SIMPLE RECALIBRATIONS

When you're querying your keyword space to get a sense of the overall link opportunities that exist, one simple though imprecise way to compare the relative opportunity size is the number of relevant opportunities in the top ten results. In order for this to work, of course, you'll have to do the same number of queries for each opportunity type. The problem with this method is in the queries themselves—though we use the queries mentioned above, many spaces have different words and variations for their different opportunity types.

Which brings us to recalibrations. Try creating your own substitutions for an opportunity type mentioned above. If our queries sound off to you, then they probably are—you know your keyword space best. Also, if you're not getting back many relevant results, your MDKW could be too narrow—try broadening them. For example, if you used "camping tents," go to "camping" and you should see more relevant opportunities appear.

Chapter 8

Link Prospecting

Link prospecting is the process of discovering potential sites for engagement designed to acquire links to your site. Link prospecting takes many forms, and can be as simple as a quick search engine query or as involved as downloading hundreds of thousands of competitor backlinks. Each method of prospecting has its pluses and minuses, as well as best practices and free/paid tools to speed up the process.

COMMON LINK-PROSPECTING METHODS

Finding link prospects is one of the core problems of link building. And usually the problem isn't in finding enough prospects. You can easily find hundreds or even hundreds of thousands of prospects by cracking open MajesticSEO.com and exporting competitor backlinks. The problem typically lies in finding link prospects that represent opportunity types that are lined up with your linkable assets. Not all the prospecting methods below answer this core link-building pain, but they are the more common methods used by link builders these days.

Link Prospecting Queries

Link-prospecting queries remain one of the most versatile and powerful "tools" for link builders. A link-prospecting query (also called a "link-building query") is a combination of keywords and advanced search operators that help you to discover sites that are likely to link to a page on your site. Link-prospecting queries are highly flexible ways to discover link prospects at large scale, and a fantastic way to quickly determine the quantity and quality of link opportunities in a given keyword space (as noted in Chapter 6).

Link-prospecting queries work because link prospects often have a common "footprint" in the content of the page or even in the URL itself. Discovering these link opportunity footprints and paring them down to only a word or two is the essence of link-prospect query design.

The chief advantage of link-prospecting queries is your ability to align your queries to discover only the link opportunities that relate to a linkable asset. This ability is your first line of prequalification, and enables you to design narrowly targeted campaigns that focus on a single asset. Thoroughly discovering all the link prospects that relate to a linkable asset is only possible with queries.

The disadvantage of queries is their ease of creation, which can encourage a cursory and unsystematic approach to querying. This unsystematic approach almost always leaves link prospects "on the table" as you move on to a different asset. Thorough link-prospect querying is fairly simple, however. A further disadvantage is link-opportunity discovery. If your site lacks a linkable asset, or you're simply unaware of a given opportunity type, you will be unable to create the appropriate queries for discovering these opportunities.

In the past we've written lists of link-building queries you can use for prospecting. The problem: There are always more queries you could possibly use.

Furthermore, you're probably only able to use a small fraction of the queries we recommend due to your linkable assets or the type of link opportunities that you're targeting with your campaign. Ultimately, we don't know your market the way you do. Knowing how to construct queries will help you hunt far more effectively in your target market than a list of queries.

Seven Types of Keywords for Link-Prospecting Queries

Mark Twain said, "The difference between the almost right word and the right word is really a large matter—it's the difference between the lightning bug and the lightning." The same certainly holds true for link-prospecting queries, which is why we've found it really helps to think about the types of words you can use. Finding just the right words will help you to prequalify your prospects, which vastly speeds up your qualification phase.

Figure 8–1 on page 53 shows a query for "lightning" combined with the intitle command for "links" that returns prequalified results for sites aggregating links related to lightning.

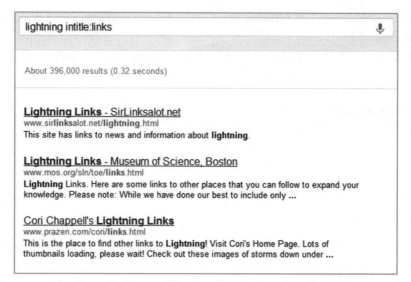

FIGURE 8–1. The Broad, General Topic of Lightning Inspired Many to Create Links Pages for Cataloging Lightning Resources. The Intitle: Links Operator Helps Find Them

FIGURE 8–2. More Specialized Keywords Like "Bioluminescence" Bring Fewer Results but More Varied Link Opportunities than General Keywords Like "Lightning"

For this exercise we'll pretend we build and sell high-performance kayaks online and from a brick-and-mortar location. Our linkable assets are an extensive guide to the best kayaking spots in the world, our blog with kayaking tips and events, and our in-house kayaking "subject matter experts," both as builders and kayakers.

1. Market-Defining Keywords (MDKWs)

As we discussed in the previous chapter, each market uses particular words to describe itself in MDKWs. What words does your target audience use to describe your industry?

For our kayaking site these terms could include:

- KayakKayakingPaddling

To find prospects for our guide to the best kayaking spots in the world we could do queries like:

- Kayak blogKayaking resourcesPlaces to kayak intitle:list

2. Customer-Defining Keywords (CDKWs)

Customer-defining keywords help you discover prospects that are geared more toward your target audience. Knowing what your customers call themselves and how they refer to fellow group members will help you discover some great prospects.

Customer-defining keywords for our kayak store could include:

- Kayaker
- Paddler
- Playboater
- "Paddle Bum"

These keywords will help you discover still more prospects who might be interested in linking to that guide to the world's best kayaking spots:

- Playboater blogKayaker resourcesPaddler vacation intitle:list

3. Product/Category Keywords (PCKWs)

Product or category keywords are the high- and mid-level terms that describe what you sell. They're useful because they can help you to uncover prospects that could otherwise go undiscovered. For example, on our kayak site we sell a few different types of kayaks. Each type of kayak has its own dedicated enthusiasts.

- Sea kayakSit on top kayakPlayboat
- CreekboatInflatable kayakFishing kayakWaveski

If you had kayaks to lend or donate for review, you could combine the above keywords with "blog," "news," "review," or even "magazine" to find people to write reviews. Add "forum" to each of the above words and you'll find people who are avid users of these types of products.

4. Industry Thought Leaders (ITLs)

Industry thought leaders—or, in our kayak case, subject matter experts—help you uncover public relations and interview opportunities in your space. Here are some names from the kayaking world (people who have given interviews on the subject):

- John Kimantas
- Tyler Bradt
- Harvey Golden

If you're looking for a market's experts, also search in Amazon, or search "MDKW book" because they often write books. You should also check YouTube for any relevant videos.

Once you know some of your industry's thought leaders, you can look for people who will respond to interviews (so you can interview them and add the content to your site) as well as people who conduct interviews so you can pitch your in-house experts!

Furthermore, you can poke around in forums and see if any thought leaders have participated there. If so, you should consider sending yours there as well. Here are some query commands:

- [ITL] interview
- intitle:"[ITL]"
- [ITL] forum

5. Competing Company Names (CCNs)

Competing company names are wonderful little footprints to track—they can show you a great deal about how your industry's reporters and bloggers treat companies similar to yours. For our kayak company, the list would include other direct competitors.

CCNs are useful in ways similar to the names of industry thought leaders. Our kayak company can see who has covered their competitors in the news, as well as which industry forums happen to discuss their competitors extensively. Furthermore, checking for reviews can show you what you're up against, plus reveal some potential link opportunities.

- [CCN] review
- [CCN] forum

- [CCN] interview
- [CCN] "guest article or post"

6. Geo Keywords (GKWs)

Geo keywords help you discover link prospects that may impact your local search rankings. Our kayak shop obviously wants to rank well locally, and in addition, by discovering and participating with local media, they will drive highly relevant referral traffic that could result in sales.

Geo keywords can include things like:

- State/province
- Region
- City
- Neighborhood
- ZIP code

Here are some ways to use geo keywords in link-prospecting queries. Our kayaking shop has monthly workshops for builders, as well as weekly one-hour training classes. It also hosts an annual bluegrass and beer festival for kayakers. We can query for sites related to the broadcast area for events like these. Both of these events are offsite assets that are ideal for geographic keyword link opportunities offered by the sites returned by the following queries:

- [GKW] events
- [GKW] blog
- [GKW] kayak blog
- [GKW] directory
- [GKW] reviews

7. Related Vertical Keywords (RVKWs)

Related or adjacent verticals are industries in your "ecosystem" that could potentially aid your prospecting and outreach efforts. These could be your suppliers' and customers' industries, perhaps. For example, here are some adjacent industries for our kayaking company:

- Canoes
- Rafting
- Biking
- Hiking
- Boat Building

Our kayaking company will want to make sure that they invite the local canoeing and rafting community to their weekly kayak training events. Bikers and hikers will probably enjoy bluegrass and beer. Further, connecting with boat-building forums, magazines, and blogs will help build links, especially if the company publishes a couple of free kayak plans (and sells others).

Some sample queries could look like:

- [RVKW] blog list
- [RVKW] news
- [RVKW] forum
- [RVKW] "guest post"
- [RVKW] "roundup"
- "[RVKW] resources"
- [RVKW] Twitter list

It would be great if Google could understand (or wanted to understand) that when I search on Customer Relationship Management intitle:"guest post" I need 500 sites likely to publish CRM-related guest posts for a client this month. Instead I'll get between three and ten decent prospects and start thinking of a new query.

As a link prospector I find this to be the core problem of using Google for prospect sourcing—the relevance of my prospects diminishes significantly after the top 10 to 20 results. And going beyond the top 20 results increases time spent qualifying without justifiable returns.

With conversion rates being what they are these days (I'm pleased by 10 to 15 percent conversion for guest posting and 3 percent for broken-link building) you can start to back into why these low numbers of usable prospects is a big problem for large-scale campaigns that have high levels of monthly link commitments.

Approaching a "fix" for this problem (besides just "more queries," which is, of course, basically the answer) requires thinking through why Google returns so few usable prospects in the top 20 for a single query. My belief is that Google intends to deliver a few "best" answers rather than to provide page after page of great possibilities. They provide a mass-use tool for the average searcher who wants to search and go, rather than a specialized research tool for someone who wants hundreds or even thousands of possible answers.

Think of the fix like this: Systematically and thoroughly alter your queries and force or "restrict" Google to provide new and still-relevant results in the top 20s that you would otherwise have never seen. Compare the command "crm guest post" to CRM intitle:"guest post." There is some domain overlap, but overall we have a large number of new domains that you should consider for placing content. There are three keys to force usable 20-result "segments" out of Google's insanely huge index:

1. Research phrases
2. Advanced operators
3. Tactic-specific footprints

ANATOMY OF A PRODUCTIVE LINK-PROSPECTING QUERY

Let's dig into each one of these and look at ways to build thorough-as-possible prospecting-query lists. Note: In our query above, CRM intitle:"guest post," "CRM" is the research phrase, "intitle:" is the advanced operator, and "guest post" is your tactic-specific footprint.

1. Research Phrase List Building

The research phrase is what directs Google in the general vicinity of your topic. It pays to spend time brainstorming and developing large lists of research phrases (though tildes can help with this immensely by "thinking" of synonyms for you).

So continuing our CRM example above, you should definitely include "customer relationship management" both with and without quotes. NOTE: I always create query batches with and without quotes as they often help float new prospects. I also tried **~crm** and **–crm,** which returned some "call centers."

Now, when I looked at the results for our CRM guest-posting query I saw that many of them were about social CRM, and a few were on small-business blogs. These also suggest avenues for prospecting so long as we can tailor content to fit the specific vertical.

So here's our working list of research phrases for CRM-related guest-post opportunities:

- CRM
- customer relationship management
- "customer relationship management"
- ~crm
- call center
- "call center"
- social crm
- "social crm"
- small business crm

- "small business" crm
- business crm

Now it's on to our list of tactic-specific footprints.

2. Tactic-Specific Footprint Lists

"Footprints" are any word or phrase that commonly occurs on the kind of page that represents a prospect to you. I call them tactic-specific footprints because ideally you keep them organized by tactic so you can reuse them in the future, and continue to add to them as you find new ones.

You can build your footprint lists by closely examining "definite yes prospects" and looking for patterns. For example, in guest posting it's common to include the phrase "about the author." It's so common that it's a solid little footprint in its own right. That said, simply "guest post," with and without quotes, are highly productive as well.

You should also check out some of Ann Smarty's guest-post footprints. Here are some of the more common guest-posting footprints to combine with the research phrases above:

- guest post
- "guest post"
- "about the author"
- "write for us"
- "blog for us"
- "guest blog for us"
- "guest blogger"
- guest blogger
- guest contributor
- "guest contributor"
- "this is a guest post"

This is by no means an exhaustive list for guest posting, but it certainly provides an excellent starting point.

3. Advanced Search Operators

If you're unfamiliar with advanced search operators, check out this list. Not all of them will be useful to link prospectors, but they're worth understanding because the best ones enable you to restrict the results enough to pinch off another five to ten useful prospects. Here are the ones I use the most:

- **intitle**: Use this operator to restrict results to documents that contain your phrase in the title tags. It's typically only conscientious or SEO-oriented webmasters who provide useful information in their title tags, so this can be a great way to filter.

- **inurl**: Similar in usage to **intitle**, **inurl** enables you to restrict your results based on what appears in the URL.

- **site**: I primarily use this operator to restrict by top level domain (TLD). For example, if a query contains **site:.edu** it will return sites with a TLD of .edu.

- **˜ (synonyms)**: The tilde operator instructs Google to return results that include synonyms to the keyword it appends. We find it particularly useful for brainstorming and to go in depth on how to use it further on.

- *** (wild card)**: The wild card is useful for "filling in the blanks" on your research phrase and footprint brainstorming. For example, you could type "guest post*" and that would include "guest post," "guest posts," "guest posting," "guest posters," etc. The wild card can combine with other operators, for example: **˜wild*** returns synonyms of words with the root "wild."

- **– (minus)**: The minus operator enables you to remove specific words that you know indicate a nonopportunity. For example, if your CRM results get cluttered with composite risk management results you could type **CRM –composite** to remove them. Minus combines with other operators.

- **intext**: **Intext** specifies that the word or phrase must appear in the text of the page.

- **"" (exact phrase)**: I use this all the time, almost without thinking about it. It's a very useful restriction that tells Google to return an exact match of the phrase in quotes.

It's important to note that not all advanced operators will be productive in combination with all the research phrases and opportunity footprints. This is where experience will help you the most. Furthermore, you'll probably find you use intitle, inurl, and tildes the most.

Next up we'll look at a huge list of combined queries so you can get a sense of what it will take to get a useful number of prospects for a CRM guest-posting campaign.

4. Queries in Action

To get a solid list of guest-posting opportunities—enough for a month at least I hope—I combined the following research phrases, operators, and footprints:

Research Phrases

- CRM
- customer relationship management
- "customer relationship management"
- ~crm
- call center
- "call center"
- social crm
- "social crm"
- small business crm
- "small business" crm
- business crm

Operators and Footprints

- guest post
- "guest post"
- "about the author"
- "write for us"
- "blog for us"
- "guest blog for us"
- "guest blogger"
- guest blogger
- guest contributor
- "guest contributor"
- "this is a guest post"
- intitle:contributor
- inurl:contributor
- intitle:guest
- inurl:guest
- intitle:"guest post"
- inurl:"guest post"
- intitle:"write for us"
- inurl:"write for us"

This netted us more than 200 queries to run. We scraped the top 10 results for each query and found 581 domains to check out. And that's only starting to scratch the surface.

THE TILDE: ADVANCED OPERATORS IN LINK PROSPECTING

The tilde is such an important and overlooked advanced operator that it deserves its own section. For beginning link prospectors, the tilde (˜) is the "synonym" operator, which, according to Bill Slawski, Google released in 2003.

This section comprises some early findings on experimenting with the tilde operator in guest-post prospecting for the health space.

Tilde Enables Synonym Discovery for Big Head Terms

Search ˜**health "guest post"** and you'll see medicine, nutrition, and fitness opportunities. If you're new to the health space you may not have thought of trying to guest post in these verticals. This saves the prospector a great deal of time.

Note that ideally you're only using big head terms that broadly define a category. Your results will vary wildly if you're looking for two-word big head phrases, so tread cautiously. It's easy to slip into irrelevance with the tilde.

Tildes Work in Conjunction With Intitle and Inurl Operators

Sweet! For example: Search **intitle:˜health** vs. **intitle:health** and you'll see far more results returned. This fact in particular excited me as it enables a higher level of specificity for where the keyword appears—this means link prospectors can be precise and fuzzy at the same time. Think of it as a sniper shotgun. The tilde did not appear to have impact within quotes, to my disappointment, e.g: "health food" vs. "˜health food" returned exactly the same results.

Combine Tilde with Negative Operator for Interesting Lateral Leaps

Run these two searches: ˜**health** and ˜**health -health**. That second query tells Google to return results that are similar to health but don't contain the word health.

In conjunction with link-building footprints these really force some leaps. The relevance certainly drops off, but they are worth including solely for the unexpected results they return.

Tilde Impact on Domain Diversity Within Guest-Posting Prospect Queries

I struggled some with how to explain or quantify the impact of using tildes in link prospecting. I went with an analysis of domain diversity.

For this comparison I took the following three research phrases: **Health**, ˜**Health** and ˜**Health -Health** and combined them with 24 guest-posting prospect footprints. I then ran the queries at a depth of 20 results (two pages deep) to see what kind of impact the tilde had on domain diversity. I used this tool for comparing domains, and it does not take into account www. vs. non-www.

Health vs. ~Health

- **Health**: 353 Unique Domains—479 Unique URLs
- **~Health**: 369 Unique Domains—477 Unique URLs
- Total Unique Domains: 480
- Intersecting Domains: 242

~Health vs. -Health ~Health

- **~Health -Health**: 356 Unique Domains—476 Unique URLs
- **~Health**: 369 Unique Domains—477 Unique URLs
- Total Unique Domains: 721
- Intersecting Domains: 4

Health vs. ~Health -Health

- **Health**: 353 Unique Domains—479 Unique URLs
- **~Health -Health**: 356 Unique Domains—476 Unique URLs
- Total Unique Domains: 695
- Intersecting Domains: 14

If you construct your queries to include all variations (which we advise at least testing) and aggregate your SERP results, you clearly get a far greater diversity of domains. This obviously doesn't mean that the results are more qualified, just that you spend less time thinking about what prospecting phrases to use.

You can try them, if you like, by combining any of the three research phrases—**Health**, **~Health** and **~Health -Health**—with **intitle:"guest post."**

Chapter 9

Competitor Backlink Prospecting

There is a simple beauty to lists of competitor backlinks. You know that each of the URLs listed has qualified itself by doing the one thing you want done for you: link out. This act alone prequalifies competitor backlink lists to some degree. If you merge lists of competitor backlinks and find the co-occurring URLs and host names, you're moving still closer to a qualified prospect list.

Besides identifying individual prospects, analyzing competitor backlinks can reveal new link opportunity types that you may have forgotten, overlooked, or not even known about. Always be on the lookout for new link opportunity types, and, if you have the assets or the resources to create the assets, be prepared to develop queries for finding more of them.

One other great way to use competitor backlinks is by looking at links to individual pages, rather than to the site as a whole. This is most useful when seeking outreach targets for a similar linkable asset that you've created.

A key difficulty with competitor backlink lists—even those with quality metrics as supplied by backlink data vendors—is an inability to quickly line up the prospects with your existing assets. You know nothing about the linking URLs and have very little way to assess why they linked in the first place.

Figuring this out for every prospect would take months to do "manually."

TOOLS FOR PULLING COMPETITOR BACKLINKS

There are a number of free and commercially available tools for pulling competitor backlinks. Here are the ones we use and recommend:

- Link Insight from AdGooroo
- Open Site Explorer
- Majestic SEO
- Ahrefs.com

FIGURE 9–1. Majestic SEO's Site Explorer

FIGURE 9–2. Ahrefs' Site Explorer

FIGURE 9–3. Open Site Explorer's Link Search Window

Chapter 10

Automating Your Link Prospecting with RSS Aggregation

O nce you've developed link-building query clusters for your ever-green linkable assets (assets that don't expire like contests or specific job openings do), it's time to set up and aggregate alerts so that you can set yourself up with a steady supply of link prospects.

SET UP SEVERAL KEYWORD-BASED RSS MONITORS

First, you need to select your source for the feed. Here are several potential sources:

- Google Alerts
- Technorati Search Query RSS
- Google Blog Search
- Trackur

Sign up if you haven't already, and begin reading about how to set up feeds with each of the tools. Then add each of your link-building queries to the tool so that it will send you corresponding pages.

You have to send your prospects some place, and ideally it's not to your email inbox. There are a number of ways to aggregate your feeds for easy qualification. Two are Google Reader and Yahoo Pipes.

By automating your prospecting using one of these online programs, you can step away for a few days, work through your other prospects, and then come back and see what has collected while you qualified and reached out to your link prospects.

Chapter 11

List-Scrape Prospecting for Link Builders

Never fear, link prospector, there remain deep wells of link prospect opportunity, even if you've queried every last prospect from Google and snatched every last link from your competitors' backlink profile. If you can make the right offer and have a ready team for outreach, then list-scrape prospecting could add a steady stream of powerful links to your portfolio.

We have the great fortune to live in an age in which webmasters aggregate and publish large lists of outbound links. It's as simple as searching Google for lists of XYZ kinds of sites, hand-picking pages with a high volume of outbound links, and "scraping" them with the same type of crawling and scraping software that Google uses to download the internet.

Often these lists are created in directory format for Adsense earnings. Sometimes these lists—a list of orchestras or a list of U.S. hospitals by state—are created by passionate curators. And of course there are the top 100+ blog lists, which you can use to search for the top 200 church blogs.

The process of list-scrape link prospecting is dead simple:

- Find lovingly crafted lists of websites
- Brainstorm a valuable, relevant pitch (this is the only hard part)
- Scrape the lists
- Remove any nonprospects

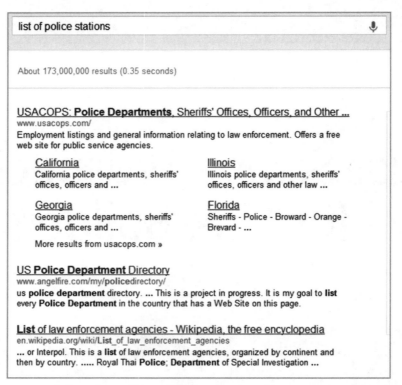

FIGURE 11–1. A Search on "List of Police Stations" Returns Several Sites that Aggregate Police Station Websites

- Scrape contact information
- Outreach, using the pitch you designed in point 2, to sites with available contact information

Oh, and yes, you can use our new Outbound Link scraper + Contact Finder tools to better automate this approach at http://tools.citationlabs.com.

LIST HUNTING

In hunting for lists, it's best to let Google's suggest function do the thinking for you. Here are some queries that have worked well for us:

- list of [institution]s
- list of U.S. [institution]s
- list of [a, b, c, etc.] websites
- list of [a, b, c, etc.] blogs
- top 10 [a, b, c, etc.] websites
- top 100 [a, b, c, etc.] blogs

I also highly recommend including the Ubersuggest tool (http://ubersuggest.org/) in your searches for lists: http://ubersuggest.org/.

Try searches like:

- list of lists
- list of websites
- list of sites
- list of websites for
- list of sites for

There are more, and your markets will probably have different names for "lists," such as "directories" or "resources," too. You're hunting for lists, but they're not always so simply and directly named.

ALIGNING YOUR PITCH WITH THE AVAILABLE LIST

If you're genuinely interested in building a campaign around list scraping, we suggest you determine your pitch *after* you've found a list that could work. It's usually less viable to start with an asset and decide to go look for lists of relevant prospects. It can happen, for sure, and you should at least look, but stay open to working with the huge lists that already exist.

Think of these lists of sites as a target market and start your brainstorming from there. What content would all the small-town hospital webmasters in the U.S. crack open their CMS and add to their websites? What critical widget is missing from the art museums of the world? Oh, you've got a killer offer for these 400 recipe and cooking sites?

And remember—in this approach you don't stop with one list. You find ALL the available lists of a target type and combine them. List scraping has the potential to be highly thorough!

One last note—be careful! This approach can cross very, very quickly into spam if you're aggressive in your outreach and don't line up the interests of your prospects, their audience, and you.

A NOTE ON BLOG LIST SCRAPING

I've found that list scraping is faster than scraping Google for popular blog subject areas (health, entertainment, etc.) with hundreds or thousands of blogs.

For example, in a search for fitness blogs, I see the following pages in the top ten results:

- 20-plus Amazing Fitness Blogs to Inspire You

- Top 20 Fitness Blogs
- Top 100 Health and Fitness Blogs

Now start looking for some fitness blog lists using the query list of fitness blogs, and we can throw several more lists on the pile:

- Favorite Fitness Blogs
- Top 100 Diet and Fitness Blogs
- TOP 100+ FITNESS BLOGS
- Five Best Fitness Blogs on the Internet
- List of Weight Loss, Health, and Fitness Blogs

From those eight URLs, I found approximately 300 fitness blogs. Even if not all of them are qualified, I can't imagine a single query in Google that would bring back 300 relevant results.

SPRAY AND PRAY?

My esteemed search marketing colleague Ken Lyons refers to this list-scraping method of prospecting and outreach as the "spray and pray" approach. It is. In an email exchange, Ross Hudgens called it "cold outreach." Yes—it's cold, quite cold.

Here are some things that can help your response rates in this approach:

- Timeliness of your message
- Aligning your offer with the needs of the publishers
- Clearly demonstrating an understanding and concern for the publisher's audience
- Recognizable, authoritative brand

Chapter 12

Link Prospect Qualification

If "Excel Hell" exists, then there must certainly be a level in it specifically for lists of link prospects. Those people who've had to find prospects worthy of outreach from lists of thousands of URLs know exactly what we're talking about. In Chapter 8 we discussed several ways to prequalify your prospects, including targeted queries designed to discover prospects in line with your assets, and finding co-occurrences among competitor backlinks.

This chapter investigates both "automated" and "manual" ways to qualify link prospects once you've gathered them for a project. We recommend you use automated methods to focus on easily measurable factors to cull the list to a manageable size. Then use a by-hand, or manual, review to further qualify and highlight the best link opportunities for the proper segment of your campaign. You can also gather contact information at the by-hand review stage, if applicable to your campaign.

QUALIFYING LINK PROSPECTS BASED ON AVAILABLE METRICS

The first place to begin attacking hundreds or thousands of prospects is with any readily available metrics. If you've used the SEOBook Firefox plugin to scrape search engine result data, you can source metrics that way. Many of the commercially available link-prospecting services have their own metrics that will enable you to qualify in a more "automated" way. Here are some more methods you can use to quickly remove prospects from large lists without actually visiting and looking at the web pages (yet).

Keyword Occurrences in URLs

If you've copied and pasted your list of link prospects into a spreadsheet program like Microsoft Excel®, one way to determine relevance is to simply search for your market-defining keywords—and potentially keywords associated with the link-opportunity type—in the URLs themselves. For example, if you've been looking for link lists on .edu sites, then the word "link" or "list" appearing in the URL is a pretty good identifier. If you want the blogs, then "blog" would be a fantastic place to start searching your spreadsheet. Any URLs that contain the keywords should be set aside for a manual review later.

Authority of Host Name or URL

Page rank (PR) remains the simplest, quickest, most scrapable metric for freely assessing the authority of a URL and its host name. We don't practice or preach chasing high page rank links, but we do firmly assert that you can make broad generalizations about a link prospect data set based on PR. If you've sourced your link prospects either from link-building queries or competitor backlink data, then sorting your list in descending order of host name PR can help you immediately spot the strongest, most authoritative sites for potential outreach. There are other authority measurements available from other link-prospecting tools that can be used to sort in much the same way.

Inbound Link Count to Host Name, Inbound Link Count to URL

Like page rank, the number of links a site has can be easily manipulated, and should never be a sole decision point for whether to establish a relationship with a site. And, like page rank, if your link prospects have been prequalified with queries or backlink co-occurrence, then inbound link count becomes a more useful number. In addition to helping you make decisions about which sites to approach for engagement, inbound link counts to nonhost name URLs can help you identify content to which your market responds well.

Distribution Metrics: Twitter Mentions, Facebook Likes, Reddit Mentions, Stumbles, Etc.

The SEOBook SEO for Firefox Toolbar also enables you to quickly pull data points such as the number of times a domain has appeared in Twitter, Facebook, on Reddit, and on StumbleUpon. These metrics are strong signals that the owners of a site are active social media participants and that they may have developed a following. These sites should certainly be set aside for further consideration, especially for content placement, interviews, and news-related engagement.

THE TOOL FOR FASTER METRICS-BASED QUALIFICATION

There's really only one tool that we've found and recommend consistently for its ease of operation and intelligent design: the SEOBook SEO for Firefox Toolbar. You have to sign up to get access, but it's highly customizable and enables you to download to spreadsheet, aggregate, and then sort your link query prospects directly from the SERPs. Many of the competitor backlink prospecting tools have their own metrics, but none of them (to our knowledge) approach the range of metrics pulled in by the SEO for Firefox Toolbar.

MAKING "BY-HAND" PROSPECT QUALIFICATIONS

At a certain point it becomes necessary to visit prospect sites by hand. We believe you should do as much work as possible to minimize the number of sites you visit by hand, as this is (one of) the most time-consuming and tedious parts of link building. It's also the point where you're likely to have the most inspiration for your campaign, so be sure to schedule ample time and be ready to capture the ideas you have.

Asset Relevance

Sometimes the presence of a link opportunity keyword in the URL can indicate possible relevance to a linkable asset. And sometimes you have to visit the page and look the site over to make sure the owner/curator is likely to be receptive to publishing a mention of your asset.

Reach and Influence Assessment

There are a number of ways to assess a site's influence and reach. To our knowledge, few of these are readily capturable in an automated, per-URL fashion. The number of blog and/or newsletter subscribers can tell you a great deal about how long the site has been around, as well as how far your linkable asset is likely to travel, should it get mentioned. The Twitter followers of the site's publisher is another decent metric, but if you're pursuing guest-post opportunities then the number of times the domain has appeared in Twitter is an even better metric of the reach of a site. Further, you should check to see if the site has badges for voting its pages up on niche social news sites. If so, search that social news site to see how often your prospect has appeared and to get an idea of how often their content has gone "hot." Go for reach and influence whenever possible!

Oops! It's a Competitor!

Sometimes competitors appear in your link prospect data sets—this can be tough to discern ahead of time, especially if you're new to a market and/or a client. Sometimes it requires a site visit to make that distinction.

At-a-Glance Site Quality

Is the design and layout pleasing, or at least not distracting? Are you bombarded with ads and AdSense links that force you to scroll in order to find the content on the page? Are there obvious misspellings and atrocious grammar? Again these could all be strong signs that this prospect should be discarded (no matter what the metrics tell you).

TOOLS FOR FASTER BY-HAND QUALIFICATION

There's only one tool that we're aware of that considerably speeds up the process of by-hand qualification. It's a free and very simple tool that we developed—the URL Reviewer Tool. Here is the step-by-step process for using the tool to speed up the final by-hand qualification of your link prospects:

1. Turn off images in your browser. You'll move faster if you have multiple tabs (or windows) open and your computer will work faster if it doesn't have to handle all those images. You can usually do this by opening your browser's settings/options.
2. Use a "URL Reviewer" tool, which opens a list of URLs in new tabs. Search for "open sites in multiple tabs."
3. Only add 10 URLs at a time at first to test the strain on your computer. If it handles 10 well, try 20, then 30. You're testing for bottlenecks here, which can occur in your RAM, your router, your internet connection, etc. You want to find the optimal speed so you can get at as many prospects as possible at a time.
4. Use Chrome, which manages RAM allocations more efficiently than FireFox, Opera, or Safari. Some link builders are wary of using Google-based products in link building, especially if they are researching link buys. If you share this concern then don't use Chrome.
5. Save yourself a mouse click and use Ctrl-W or Command-W to close tabs.
6. Only make a mark for confirmed, definite prospects in your spreadsheet. Once you've finished going through your list you can sort by that column and mark

all the others as "Not Prospects." Your nonprospects are at least as valuable as your prospects—they will help you qualify prospects even more quickly in the future.

Using these methods, focused link builders can hand-qualify up to 250 URLs an hour. Garrett, who suffers at times from ADD and inspiration-induced reveries, can often plow through 100 or so. Your times will vary.

55 LINK-OPPORTUNITY QUALIFIERS

This list of 55 qualifiers should help to get your brain turning regarding metrics and methods for qualifying your link prospects.

24 Automated Qualifiers

1. Keywords appear in target URL
2. Keywords appear in target URL title tag
3. Keywords appear in H1 tags
4. Keyword occurrences in body text
5. Keyword occurrences in Meta keywords and description
6. Number of outbound links on target URL
7. Number of inbound links to target URL
8. Number of inbound links to domain
9. Followed/NoFollowed outbound links
10. Competitor URLs
11. Excessive AdSense placements
12. PageRank of URL
13. PageRank of domain
14. Domain age
15. Page type (social network, blog, answers page, forum, links page, etc.)
16. Number of comments in comment threads
17. Inbound links from news sites, .edus or .govs
18. Inbound links from blogs and other sites within your prospect set
19. Forum signature inbound links
20. Inbound links from niche/industry news sites
21. Inbound links from industry groups and organizations
22. Social media inbound links (Twitter, StumbleUpon, Reddit, Delicious, etc.)
23. Social media/industry group badge outbound links
24. Page type (blog, review page, links page, etc.)

31 By-Hand Qualifiers

1. Is there genuine relevance between the page and the page you're building links to?
2. Is it a previously unidentified competitor?
3. Is the text human generated?
4. Are there excessive, obtrusive ads?
5. What motivated the current links on the target URL?
6. Recent posts, recent site updates, updated copyright date?
7. At first pass, does the text look correct in grammar and spelling?
8. What is the design and image quality?
9. How thorough and well-tended does the resources/links page seem?
10. Is there more than one link page?
11. When was the last update?
12. Is the site owner/moderator easily accessible by email or phone?
13. Is there a comments box?
14. What is the quality of comments and conversation there now?
15. Does it contain discussion related to your product or service?
16. Is there an established community evident in comments or an adjunct forum?
17. Are there Q/A forms on the site?
18. Does it have strong content?
19. Does the site have editors?
20. Are there links out to other known influencers?
21. Does the site contain written reviews?
22. Email newsletter or other signs of reach and distribution
23. "In The News" section with quotes by major newspapers and industry publications
24. Person's name is the URL
25. Industry analyst/consultant site
26. Niche industry news coverage site
27. Robust commenting community with a great deal of response from author
28. Writing about recent industry news and developments
29. Obviously attends conferences
30. Multiple media formats
31. You've seen this URL on multiple blogrolls

Chapter 13

What Is Link Trust?

O n the web, where engines index URLs by the billions (the good, the bad and the ugly), signals of trust, merit, and intent of source will be crucial to any search result, including a personalized search result.

Signals of trust, merit, and intent of source can be determined in a couple of ways with an algorithm that looks at onsite or offsite signals, or without an algorithm at all, using offline factors (rarely discussed, by the way).

So links, citations, inclusions, and connections, along with confidence, intent, credibility, and veracity aren't going anywhere, because what other signals are there?

Seriously, if you had a billion dollars and wanted to start a search engine, what signals is your big fancy algorithm going to measure in order to produce useful results?

What's likely true is the sources of all signals are getting more and more algorithmic scrutiny, and end users play a larger role in this process in many ways. The links you depend on for both traffic and rank better be bulletproof, and not a house of cards waiting to crumble. If your link-building tactics and targets have not been wisely chosen, the day will come (or already has) when you will not be happy. The value of certain types of links cannot be underestimated.

Why? Because they are so hard to get, and are based on a decision made by a person (as in, um, personalized) who is a passionate subject expert. They don't have to be a Ph.D. or a librarian or a famous blogger. They just have to be able to provide algorithmic confidence signals. And you need to know what those signals are. I know what many of them are because I've sat in front of a computer screen for way many years studying it, working at it, over and over and over.

The ability to identify who and what a true influencer is, and why, is crucial for both broad and narrow topics. For any topic. It's just as important as knowing how to interact with each one of them in the right way in order to get what you seek.

At a search industry conference back in 2002, during a Q&A session, a panelist (me?) was challenged for being too cautious and unrealistic with his tactics. The panelist had just told the entire room that link-building tactics, like mass directory submission, or article syndication/submission, or indiscreet reciprocal linking, or press releases, or paid links, and even some forms of linkbait, were all doomed to failure sooner or later, that any website basing its long-term success on such tactics would fail.

It would be unfair to point fingers at any one company in particular, because to some extent we have all helped perpetuate the link-building myths that Google innocently fueled when it first gave us PageRank. At the same time, I find it hard to believe anyone who earns their living by building links is really surprised by what has happened over the years and continues to happen here in 2013. For example, the devaluing of directory links. Are you really shocked that Google no longer thinks a link from link-o-matic, link-to-my-loo, and LinksForNoGoodReason.com are of any value?

How about deep links inserted inside articles and then syndicated to hundreds of other sites? It's junk. The only thing you should be shocked about is how long it's taken the search engines to devalue this spammy link-building approach. It's the same with reciprocal link networks. Or blog link networks. In fact, any linking tactic not driven by merit but rather by deception cannot be trusted.

Many link-building services confuse a steady stream of new clients to be an indicator that they are effective link builders. They are wrong.

Google's focus on trusted sources is your worst nightmare. At the heart of the trusted link model is the word *trust*. But the mistake being made is missing the true origin of that trust. It is never the page itself that is trustworthy. Neither is it the domain, nor is it the IP block or the number of co-hosted websites present or some other silly metric. Trust originates with the steward of the content. The page editor. The author. The curator. Trust originates from people, and manifests itself on the web as links. The engine that figured that out first was Google, and others followed.

My favorite saying is as accurate today as it was in the 1990s: The engines already know how to count links. What they don't know, and what they will get better at, is knowing which of the links they have counted actually matter.

SPOTTING SIGNS OF TRUST

What signs does one look for when seeking a good link target site? There is a generic answer and a specific answer.

Generic answer: A good link target will be different for every site you are seeking links for.

Specific answer: Let's say the site you are seeking links for is devoted to everything about the history of jazz music, like the one shown in Figure 13–1: www.apassion 4jazz.net.

FIGURE 13–1. If This Was The Site You Were Seeking Links For . . .

FIGURE 13–2. Then This Site Is a Great Target Site to Get a Link From

An example of an absolutely high quality and trusted target site would be http://www.lib.unc.edu/music/research/blues.html, a page of links for blues music research sponsored by the University of North Carolina, featured in Figure 13–2.

Why? Many reasons. First, always look for the intent of the target site. In the example above, the intent of a university music web guide is pretty evident. That site isn't there to sell links, barter links, swap links, trade links, triangulate links, or any other silly link scheme. The intent has nothing to do with any search engine. That site exists as a resource to help people. A link from that site and others like it sends incredibly powerful signals of trust to the search engines.

The beauty of this is it doesn't take many such signals/links to get to a point where the engines will then, by extension and association, trust apassion4jazz.net as well.

And as the search result on the following page shows, they obviously do.

FIGURE 13–3. Search Result for "History of Jazz Music" Shows Apassion4jazz.net, Thanks to Its High-Trust Content Links, at the Top

Chapter 14

Relationship Building

Preciprocation, from Relationships to Links, and Developing Your Content Promotion Network

There is a tendency among SEOs to have a "drop-and-dash" mentality when it comes to links. This is why there are so many comment and forum spamming bots, long lists of sites where you can snag social media profile links, and a huge market for paid links. This chapter focuses on philosophies and tactics that, though time consuming, will ultimately result in a steady flow of high-value inbound links that your competitors won't be able to duplicate.

Good reciprocation and relationship-building targets include reporters, bloggers, industry experts who publish consistently, even respected and prolific forum posters. From the link prospects you qualify, look for active sites and individuals mentioned frequently in social media, as well as those that have established authority.

If there's a "secret" to our biggest successes in link building (outside of dramatically reducing prospecting and qualification time), this chapter contains it.

THE PRECIPROCATION CONCEPT

The "preciprocation" concept is simple: Promote the best content of others (especially including your link prospects) before they ask for it via links from your site and placed content, votes, newsletter mentions, tweets, or whatever platform or medium you have at your disposal. Link out lavishly to deserving content, even from competitors, if appropriate. Use followed links. Expect nothing in return, though certainly do occasional outreach to let folks know that you appreciated and cited their work.

Preciprocation provides several advantages:

- By continually watching for and promoting great industry content, you will know what you should be aspiring to in your content creation.
- Your audience will come to trust you as an expert curator of industry content. Though the content isn't yours, your "brand" will still pass along a bit as the referrer.
- You keep tabs on what your competitors are doing in the content marketing and social media arena.
- The experts creating the content you promote will, in some cases, reciprocate by promoting your content to their network.
- Some experts may be relied upon to link to you with anchor text best suited to your SEO goals.
- The experts and other publishers you promote will be more open to interviews, surveys, and other highly linkable content collaborations.

The disadvantages of preciprocation are:

- Not every market contains a layer of active, expert publishers (such as bloggers), who are the link prospects most likely to respond to this method.
- It's a lot of work, requiring dedicated daily work of about an hour or so.
- It takes a long time to get "rolling" to the point where you're genuinely impacting your chances of increasing links.
- If you're pushy or expectant in your requests for promotion of your content, you will come off as rude, even if you've been preciprocating for weeks or months.

BUILDING PRECIPROCATED RELATIONSHIPS INTO LINKS

Once you have begun warming up your link targets through preciprocation, you can start to formulate ideas for turning these contacts into links. We recommend that you do this primarily through content that, again, promotes your link targets while adding new information and new value to your industry's thought space.

Here are some core concepts that illustrate how to develop your preciprocated relationships into content and links:

- *Good Ol' Content Promotion*: If you already have expert-grade content on your site and it hasn't gotten much industry attention, a simple mention to a few of your preciprocated contacts could result in links. Because the relationships are already warmed up, they're more likely to spend a minute considering your request!

- *Top 100 (Blog Posts, Twitter Users, PDFs, Podcasts, etc.) of 20XX*: If you create content on your site that highlights the experts in your space that you've preciprocated, they are likely to help you promote it. Sometimes this will be through tweets, and sometimes through links.

- *Expert Publisher Group Interview*: Ask great questions of a large group of industry experts (including those competitors with whom you've developed rapport and respect) and you're sure to create content that gets others thinking and sharing. Plus the experts themselves will benefit by promoting the content.

- *The "Writing Assignment"*: Create an interesting and engaging writing project and ask your preciprocated experts to publish their assignment on their site—be sure to link to their assignment from the assignment announcement page, which is on your site.

FIGURE 14–1. Rae Hoffman Publishes an Annual "Expert Interview" on Link Building, Which in Turn Helps Her Site Attract Links and Publicity

- *Promoting Your Customers*: This old PR technique works well for link building. Source, share, and promote their stories and expertise, and you'll earn links from them and their networks.
- *Solicit Expert Content*: Some experts will want to use your blog as a place to reach a new audience with content (and earn a new link or two). Consider opening up your platform to content placement from others and they are likely to help promote it for you.

In the link-building campaign templates (see Chapter 18) you'll find these concepts developed in actionable detail.

DEVELOP YOUR CONTENT PROMOTION NETWORK (TO TAP INTO OTHERS' NETWORKS)

The more reach you develop for your organization—the more RSS/newsletter subscribers, the more followers and friends, the more votes you can wrangle on niche social news sites, the more forums you contribute to, the stronger the forum you create on your site—the farther your content will go and the more links it will earn. From a tactical perspective this will require you to be an active publisher in multiple mediums, and it requires dedicated daily effort from at least one employee with a strong "curatorial" eye.

You will find, as your distribution network grows, that you will earn links and mentions from the people paying attention to you. Furthermore, you will find it much easier to establish relationships with other major players in your space who have created similar networks. As you discover and promote rising stars in your market space you will earn the appreciation of future giants. Developing your link distribution network is a long-term project, and something that you do gradually as you discover and qualify new link prospects, "preciprocate" them, publish new content, and conduct outreach for it.

Here are some of the pillars of a content distribution network:

- *Twitter/Facebook*: Probably the simplest channel to set up and get running for the purposes of promoting your industry experts' best content.
- *Company Blog*: Fairly simple to set up, the real challenge comes in developing a sustainable and effective content strategy. Starting with some of the concepts from Chapter 5 will help you build links.
- *Email Newsletter*: While not a direct link-building tool, an email newsletter filled with great content gives you more reach and impact for your content. Plus it becomes a way to preciprocate—and to say thank you—to your link prospects.
- *Forum/Community Platform*: Participate (answer and ask questions) in the important ones in your industry, but also consider launching your own as a means to develop links and embed yourself more powerfully in your market.

FIGURE 14–2. Larry Chase's Newsletter, *Web Digest for Marketers*, Is the Ultimate Example of Newsletter-as-Marketing Tool

■ *Niche Social News Sites*: Discover the niche social news sites most relevant to your target audience, and if there isn't one, consider creating one and adding it to your site. Like a forum, this project is not to be undertaken lightly or without resources to promote and build it.

While your content distribution network will earn you links organically, it's important to remember that each independent channel you develop is its own linkable asset. There will be new link opportunity types you can acquire links from as you launch new channels.

OVERPRECIPROCATING: THE DANGERS OF ALWAYS BEING THE "PLATFORM"

As this chapter demonstrates, we are firm believers in promoting the content contributions of an industry's experts. This is because we've seen the impact it's had on our business, our links, and our relationships in our own space. There is a time and place when you can "over" reciprocate and get a little too wrapped up in promoting others and not seeking ways to add value to the conversation that comes directly from your experience.

We generate a great deal of our business leads through publishing unique content in leading industry publications. We once did a series of group interviews on a leading industry blog and discovered that our lead flow stopped entirely. Why? We stopped being the experts and let the spotlight shine on our peers in the industry. The upside, of course, is that the experts (including competitors) we interviewed have remained friendly if not become our out-and-out supporters.

This entire chapter is about shining the spotlight on others. Just remember that the platform you're building for yourself must benefit you, too, and the best way to do this is by publishing fantastic content that helps your industry solve its pains in new and more efficient ways.

Chapter 15

Analyzing Market Pains to Create Highly Linkable Content

I n the previous chapter we discussed preciprocation and warming up your market; this chapter expands on the warning at the end of Chapter 14: Be helpful, promote your link prospects, but don't always be the platform for others to tap dance on. You have to demonstrate your expertise—you have to add your own unique value and voice to the conversation. This chapter will help you identify exactly what kinds of content you should be creating in order to not only attract links from your prospects, but to also be sure to get some real-life conversions with your content.

Chapter 5, the linkable assets chapter, includes a good overview of what to look for on your site and in your market but doesn't go into content creation; this chapter does, with an emphasis on written content, as that's what we're most familiar with. We highly recommend you experiment with the medium that works best for you and your organization's strength. If you have developers, your content can and should look like free web tools that relate to your market. If you have graphic designers (and access to unique data and talented data interpreters), then perhaps it's infographics.

HOW-TOS, GUIDES, AND OTHER INFORMATIONAL WONDERS FOR DIYERS AND CURIOUS PROSPECTS

Fresh and up-to-date how-to content has and will have eternal appeal in a market. That's what makes it the standby for the linkable content creator. How-to content guides readers through a process for achieving a specific goal that's relevant or related to the target market. It's through this type of content that link builders (or your content strategists and PR folk) work to establish your company's experts as thought leaders and people of influence. This content travels in all sorts of media wrappers, from PDFs to podcasts, to videos, to tweets. A small selection is shown in the screen shot in Figure 15–1.

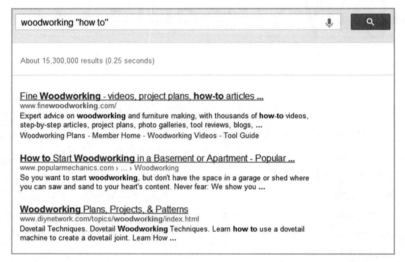

FIGURE 15–1. In The Search Results for "Woodworking 'How To,'" We Find Plans, Forums, Videos, and Tool Guides—all Valuable Content

Effective how-to content solves a market's pains. If you're already familiar with your market, you probably know the core pains. You will still be surprised at pains you weren't aware of if you conduct a "pain-point survey." If you're new to a market space then this survey will be invaluable. Note that this survey only looks at pains that content creators have addressed!

A How-To Survey for Market Pain-Point Analysis

You will need to refer back to your market-defining keywords (or MDKWs).

Your MDKWs help you guide your queries toward the information that will be most useful to you. Start by combining MDKWs with the types of words listed below. Your market is likely to have different words to describe helpful content, and it could make sense for you to search in Twitter, Reddit, Facebook, or other social sites where content related to your market is shared.

Here are some sample queries:

- [MDKW] how to
- [MDKW] advice
- [MDKW] tips
- [MDKW] process
- [MDKW] tutorial
- [MDKW] about
- [MDKW] recommended
- [MDKW] recommendations
- [MDKW] tricks
- [MDKW] basics
- [MDKW] guide
- [MDKW] definitive guide
- [MDKW] hints
- [MDKW] what you need to know
- [MDKW] ideas

Also play with these (but only concentrate on titles!):

- [MDKW] article
- [MDKW] book
- [MDKW] video
- [MDKW] podcast
- [MDKW] PDF

Begin with some by-hand queries and check the top ten for one or two MDKWs. If you find queries with lots of unique, decent looking content (just by looking at the SERPs—don't visit pages yet), set these queries aside for a larger batched query.

Conducting How-To Oriented Pain-Point Analysis

Now you have, laid out for you in plain numbers, the most commonly occurring phrases in the SERPs for the how-to content in your market. This is your starting point for creating a pain-point framework. This pain-point analysis should be fairly stable—core pains in a market rarely change. That's part of what unifies the market. Here's how to lay things out and start getting a sense for the most important types of information in your space.

1. Make a list of the distinct phrases that stand out.
2. Think about each phrase you extract as if it were going to be an entire section of your site, or a category on your blog.
3. Be as thorough as possible, and lay your preconceptions aside as much as possible.
4. Once you've assessed the main phrases that define the pains in your market, you can run each pain phrase in place of the [MDKW] queries above to flesh out each category.

You can use your pain-point analysis in a number of ways. Here are some thoughts:

- Identify what information is missing or poorly presented in your market.
- Create a content calendar for your writers.
- Identify interview questions, or general interview directions, for experts.
- Create a content site or site section architecture.
- Aggregate the best and most-linked pieces of how-to content for each pain point.
- Develop free, web-based tools or downloads targeting specific pains and create content describing how and when to use them.

IDENTIFYING LINKABLE CONTENT IN YOUR MARKET

The process outlined in the how-to discussion above provides a broad and informational look at what causes your market pain, and therefore what your market cares about. It's reasonable to assume that if you solve these pains with content, your site will attract links over time. There's more than one way to analyze content in a market, though. This section looks at how to identify and analyze the most linkable content in your market. This will help give you a sense of what factors matter to the linkers in your space (assuming your space has a community of organic linkers).

Further, this analysis will help you to weed out which market pains matter the most, and which pains are created by content farms to respond to emerging keyword demand (these could be useful too, but aren't likely to have links).

PROCESS AND TOOLS FOR IDENTIFYING LINKABLE CONTENT

At its core, this process revolves around analyzing inbound links to individual pages and *not* the site as a whole. Why? This leads you directly to important and valued pieces of content (they were cited by others), and it gives you a list of ready prospects when you create better content. Like the how-to analysis above, there are not yet any tools that execute this process on a systematized basis, so you will have to do it by hand.

This is a fairly lengthy process, but well worth the time invested.

Identify the Top Publishers in Your Market

In Chapter 4 we discussed queries for identifying blogs and news sites. Add in a few of the how-to queries above and you can use these queries to assess the strongest content and publishing players in your market. Start with queries like these:

- [MDFK] blogs
- [MDFK] news
- [MDFK] trade publication
- [MDKW] how to
- [MDKW] tips

And then . . .

1. Make sure SEO for Firefox is fully engaged—you will be extracting URLs from the SERPs of your favorite search engine.
2. Make sure your search engine of choice is returning 20 results at a time.
3. Run your first query and then extract the results (be sure to save it in a meaningful, easy-to-remember way).
4. Repeat until you've run through all of your queries.
5. Paste ONLY the URLs into the Host name and URL Occurrence Counter
6. Check, by hand, the top occurring host names and URLs—these are most likely to be your industry's top publishers.

Analyze the Top Publishers' Most-Linked Pages

Now that you have a rough idea of your top publishers, you can begin to analyze their most-linked pages. You can and should use this process to analyze your top competitors to see which of their pages have attracted the most links—not only will you discover their linkbait and linkable content, but you'll uncover pages with paid links pointing to them as well. Figure 15–2 on page 96 shows what this process looks like.

1. Take your list of top publishers and run them, one by one, through Ahrefs.com, Link Insight, Open Site Explorer, or MajesticSEO.com.
2. Examine the top 50 or so results for each site.
3. Explore URLs that appear to be informational, or contain something other than sales content.
4. Record URLs of note, along with their link count and title of the content in a spreadsheet.

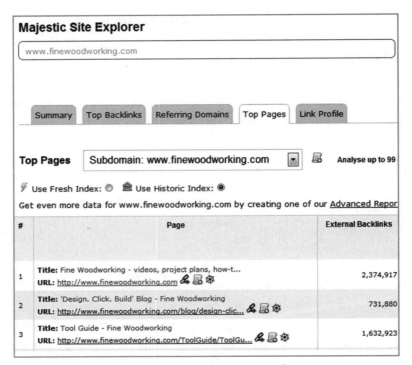

FIGURE 15–2. Majestic Site Explorer

5. Repeat for each publisher, and then sort your spreadsheet by the inbound link count column. Now you can see the URLs in your market's top publishers that have attracted, earned, or begged for the most links in your market. Here are some of the things you can start to identify now:
   - Pain addressed (how does it line up with your pain map?)
   - Target audience (knowledge level of target audience, reading level, etc.)
   - What is the content type? (article, pdf, video, podcast, infographic, etc.)
   - How is the content structured?

There's an added bonus to this sort of analysis, too—if you pull the backlinks to these top URLs, using Ahrefs.com or Open Site Explorer, you have some fairly well qualified targets for outreach as you begin to create content of your own.

REMEMBER: LINKABLE CONTENT CAN GENERATE CONVERSIONS, TOO!

In a perfect world—which you as a link builder should be striving for, obviously— linkable, shareable content also generates conversions of some fashion or other. Whether newsletter subscribers, ebook downloads, ad clicks, or even sales, your linkable content should be moving folks along a funnel. The great part is, though, if your linkable content can convert, you know you're generating *relevant* content. There are some link-builders who specialize in irrelevant linkbait. It attracts links and impacts SERPs, but chances are good that this impact won't last forever.

If every link you earn brings in targeted traffic to content that leads folks along a funnel toward increased value interactions with your brand, then you're way ahead of the game. SERP impact is your gravy. The good news is that all your how-to pain point and linkable content research has prepared you with a massive list of topics and potential titles. Your job now is discovering how to work your company's brand and buy cycle into the topics.

Here are some types of conversions you can drive with content:

- PDF Downloads
- Newsletter Sign-Ups
- Community Sign-Ups
- Free Tool Usage
- Webinar Sign-Up
- Social Follow
- RSS Subscription
- Increased Time on Site
- Sale

ENGAGING YOUR INTERNAL THOUGHT LEADERS AND SUBJECT MATTER EXPERTS

Unless you, the link builder, are your organization's subject matter expert, you're going to have to work with the folks in your organization who *are*. Content that enables an audience to gain access to these subject matter experts is more likely to result in links. Primarily, you will be engaging them with interviews, though if you have a strong team, willing experts, and the blessings of the management, you could have them write—or assist them in writing—the pain-based linkable content you've identified. Furthermore, your organization's subject matter experts may have already developed their own online platforms. There could be folks in your organization who have relevant followings already that you could ask to become more involved in your linkable content creation. If your CEO's already on Twitter, by all means ask him to tweet about your latest guides to accomplishing more with less!

TIP-BASED CONTENT—HOW TO RESEARCH, SCALE, AND PROMOTE

Tips are the smallest documentable unit of "how to" do something. Their presence—or absence—within a target market's SERPs provide phenomenal opportunities for link strategists and other content marketers. Here's a proposed definition of "tips" for marketers, and ideas and direction for link strategists and other content marketers on how to utilize tip-based content to meet marketing goals.

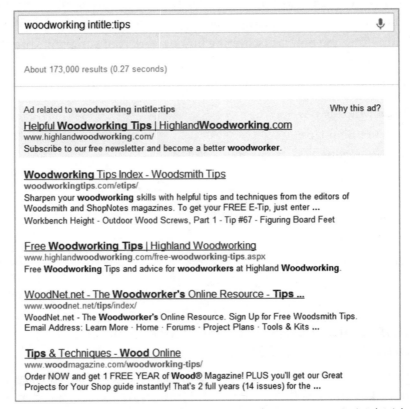

FIGURE 15–3. An Example of Google's "Intitle" Operator Paired with the Keyword "Woodworking"

Importance of Tips to Marketers

You know what a tip is, but they've become so mundane, you may not have examined them at close range. Tips are tiny concept vessels for preserving and passing along distinct units of practical advice from subject matter experts. From the information seeker's perspective, tips provide a perceived shortcut to subject matter mastery, and provide a solution to their painful inability.

By providing a tip that enables someone to complete a task, the marketer builds trust and creates further promotion opportunity—from links, to shares, to downloads, to sign-ups. When researching a space, "tips" can include other units of knowledge such as "steps," "checklists," "worksheets," "guidelines," and more.

Four Tips on Understanding the Significance of Tips within a Vertical

Tips tell marketers a great deal about a given vertical, its publishers, its audiences, and their pains. As you hone your tip-research skills, here are four things you can look for.

1. The presence of tips in your vertical demonstrates that there is task-based information demand. Even if your content isn't tip-based, the presence of tips indicates that your market needs information on how to execute relevant tasks. Gathering and organizing tips will help you understand the range of information demand as well as the various tasks that are problematic for your audience.

2. The absence of tips indicates subject matter mastery may require understanding principles rather than following tips. From a content perspective, this will require from you and your writers more effort to create successful content. Assuming you're an agency specializing in tip-based content creation, you may be doing the principle-to-tip distillation based on conjecture or—better still—interviews with subject matter experts.

3. The absence of tips indicates a content opportunity. Even if subject matter expertise in a vertical requires the understanding of principles, or even an advanced college degree, years in the field, passing a bar exam, etc., the absence of tips means that a smart content marketer can begin the work of distilling general principles into distinct, task-oriented directives. You will have difficulty in sourcing your tips, but being "first to market" with tips can create significant value for a company.

4. Identify any tip gaps as they overlap with business objectives. Markets with tips are likely to still have "tip gaps." Being able to identify these gaps—especially as they overlap with your content marketing objectives—requires a systematic inventory and categorization of existing tips.

Three Tips for Research and Categorization

Digging into a vertical's tips provides a rich well of direction and source material for your own tip-based content.

1. *Inventory tips by combining your subject matter phrases with tip-discovery stems.* Your subject matter phrases are typically non-pay-per-click, big-head keywords that

describe your target market, its various practitioners, and/or core concerns that can serve as a root for your tip queries in Google. Tip-discovery query stems are words like:

- "tips"
- "ideas"
- "techniques"
- "ways to"
- "how-tos"
- "advice"

2. *Verticals typically have unique names for types of "tips."* "Recipes" are common collections of tips in the cooking vertical; "drills" are ideas for exercises that sport coaches can implement at practice; and "lesson plans" are a sort of education recipe for teachers to follow in class. It's vital that you identify any standard, codified groupings of information in your vertical!

3. *Create a "tip-lopedia," or tip inventory, for your vertical's body of tip-based knowledge.* If you're working in a vertical for the long term, or at least for a 6- or 12-month content-oriented engagement, it makes sense to build your own tip-lopedia for cataloging and categorizing all the tips and their sources in your vertical. Then, when it comes time to create content, you can parcel out your tips based on the requirements of the given piece. When you've thoroughly collected tips from a vertical, you can more easily discover appropriate categories and groupings for them. These categorizations themselves can become a value-add to a given body of knowledge.

Five Tips for Scalable and Unique Tip-Based Content

Simply rewriting tips doesn't help differentiate your content—or add anything new to your vertical. Here are some ways to use existing tips as a starting point rather than an end goal.

1. *"Unpack" and/or "debunk" tip clichés in your vertical.* As you build your vertical's tip-lopedia spreadsheet, track the number of times a tip is mentioned or suggested. The most frequently mentioned tips can potentially be split into even smaller tips, or at least written about with more depth, deliberation, and care. It may also be possible or useful to debunk, disprove, or in some way debate the most frequently promoted tips in a vertical.

2. *Many subject matter experts haven't reduced tips and advice to their smallest form.* Your vertical's most prominent and important subject matter experts—your niche celebrities—have probably come up with some amazing, if not fully articulated,

tips. It's also probable that they haven't broken these tips down to their smallest possible form.

3. *Tips and tip categories can serve as a basis for group interviews.* Knowing the most regularly published tips can be a great place to start an interview with your niche expert celebrities. Ask them to debunk the common tips, or to provide their unique spin on that particular tip. You can also ask, "What tips besides these most common tips would you recommend?"

4. *Tips can serve as a basis for infographics or other "utility enhancers."* Providing new wrappers for old or standard tips can give your content new life in a vertical. Can making tips printable in some way improve their utility? Can you turn your tip-lopedia into a simple fact-finding or diagnosis application?

5. *If forum-based tip sharing happens frequently in your vertical, this is a huge opportunity for tipsourcing.* While forums and other social media sites can provide the most useful, actionable tips, they are often poorly organized, incompletely explained, and have no "architecture" to them.

Four Tips for Promoting Tip-Based Content

Tip-based content can earn links, shares, and other citations with no promotion. Tip-based content can also perform poorly even with extensive promotion. Here are some tips on promotion:

1. *Cite and notify your tip sources.* You are rewriting, rearticulating, and reorganizing their tips to the point that they are no longer recognizable to their originators. However, citing your sources provides an anchor of trust and reliability to your content, and provides you with a promotion opportunity as well when you write to the esteemed subject matter expert to let them know that you referenced them in your humble work.

2. *Target roundup writers.* If your vertical has roundup writers, then these are some of the first folks you should target for mention, share, or link requests.

3. *Distribute it yourself.* Tweet it, share it, put it on your homepage, link to it from guest posts, include the URL in relevant comments, and add it to your monthly email newsletter.

4. *Make sure your content targets a conversion.* Tip-based content conversions can include things like signups, downloads, installs, follows, friends, shares, links, and even sales if you have ebooks or other content for sale.

Chapter 16

Link Acquisition

Link acquisition is the process of conducting outreach designed to induce people or sites to publish links to your content (and, in our methodology, without paying them). Link acquisition is sometimes referred to as "link begging," but this is a misnomer. In effective link acquisition, you always—*always*—illustrate the value of your linkable asset within the context of the needs of the publisher's target audience. Our most effective link acquisition emails typically don't even use the word "link" in them.

DESIGNING THE PITCH: BEFORE SENDING YOUR LINK ACQUISITION EMAILS

The first and most important stage of link acquisition is in your pitch design. Effective pitch design also relies upon a thorough linkable asset inventory (so you know what you're pitching) and effective link prospecting and qualification (so you know who you're pitching to, and why).

Relevance First: Aligning Your Assets with the Link Opportunity Types

You have a list of prospects, but do you know which of your linkable assets lines up with their interests, with their audience, with their editorial agendas? For scalable and effective link-building campaigns, we recommend that you organize the campaign with assets at the core. The more relevant your asset is to the prospect, the higher your conversion rates will be.

WARMER RELATIONS: SENDING "PRECIPROCATION" SIGNALS IN EVERY EMAIL

There's a reason this book goes from link prospect qualification to building relationships, and not directly to link acquisition. Preciprocation is one of the strongest indicators you can give someone that you're invested in moving your industry forward with enthusiasm and optimism. Furthermore, it shows that you're listening to them, which is one of the most powerful ways to open up the hearts and minds of your industry's publishers. We recommend that you (*and* challenge you to) build preciprocation, in some way, into every email you send.

For example, if you haven't contacted someone yet, you could send preciprocation signals like this:

> I really enjoyed your piece on X. In fact, I mentioned it in our email newsletter, to my Twitter followers, and added it to this massive roundup of our industry's top resources (URL). Check it out and if you think it's worthy, please mention it to your readers! Also, I'd like to interview you for an upcoming article—are you open to answering some questions for my readers?

If this is your second or third contact you can tone down on the preciprocation some, but always remember to indicate your future willingness to help out. If you know your expert is writing a book, for example, your letter might be more along the lines of:

> Hey [Contact Name]!
>
> Just writing to let you know that we dropped another little bomb on the X industry ;) It's really picking up steam on Twitter and causing a lot of discussion. Check it out and let me know what you think! [insert your URL] Also, let me know when you're done with that ebook so I can tell my readers about it!

DEMONSTRATING CONCERN FOR THEIR AUDIENCE'S NEEDS

When promoting your own content to publishers, one of the strongest ways to signal that you're worth listening to is by demonstrating concern for their readers. If the publisher is a good and worthy steward of your industry's community—and he will be because you've prospected and qualified well—then the readers will be *his* primary concern.

Of course, these folks are going to be few and far between. However, they are the most valuable and influential links and relationships you'll find in your space because they will have developed *trust* from their readers. And you can be sure they will have developed trust from the search engines as well.

Another way to demonstrate concern for the reader is by expressing how your readers and site visitors have responded to your content (whether by links, mentions in Twitter, actual written responses you've received, etc.). This shows you've been listening. Finally, by using language like "If you think your readers could learn from it," or "Because your readers responded so well to X," you demonstrate that you, too, care about readers.

It's always best to err on the side of concern for readers. If the publisher is publishing a blog or industry news site, you could try saying "visitors" instead of "readers."

SUGGESTING "MENTIONS" OR "SHARING" INSTEAD OF REQUESTING LINKS

The word "link" has gotten some bad connotations of late. You have to remember that publishers not only get bombarded with link-exchange spam, but there's Google pushing the "No Follow" tag and threatening to end a website's supply of organic traffic if that site does any "unnatural linking."

And think about it—the word "link" itself is abstract, too technical, and doesn't convey the actual value that your content will bring to other publishers' readers. No one wants to link. They want to share valuable content. They want to be the conduit for someone's life-changing (or business-process-changing) epiphany. They want to earn still more trust and adulation from their readers. Asking for a "link" just mucks up their thinking about this goal, and makes them suspicious of your true motives.

Therefore we recommend—in most situations involving content promotion—you stay away from the word "link." Use words like "share," "mention," "let your readers/ followers know," etc. This language also leaves them open to share your URLs in the ways they see fit.

HOW MUCH CUSTOMIZATION IS ENOUGH FOR YOUR OUTREACH?

In the early stages of preciprocation, there's no level of customization that is too much, especially for the most influential publishers and prospects in your space. Your first few contacts with your link prospects should, ideally, be as customized as possible.

Ideals are one thing, and the reality of contacting 250 publishers, or even 2,500, is a circumstance that calls for some time spent adjusting your ideals. At a certain point, you're going to have to resort to using some templates. A decent rule of thumb is that the more preciprocation you build into your outreach email, the less customization you have to do.

To illustrate, we found that when we asked people to participate in interviews they were more likely to mention our content to their readers, especially when the content on our site we asked them to mention highlights them in some way. Further, the more you've already mentioned and promoted a prospect or even someone who already links to you, the more you've already earned their trust, the more likely you can dash off a quick template request for an action on their part that benefits you. As in all relationships, this should be done sparingly.

Customize your engagements as much as possible, and in cases where you have to resort to templates, make sure you're building in some strong reasons for them to listen to your pitch and respond by mentioning to you.

SENDING YOUR EMAILS: GULP . . . EXECUTING THAT IRREVOCABLE MOMENT

Clicking "Send" on a link-request email is an exciting and terrifying moment. It's worth listening to your gut instincts the moment before you send an email because it may lead you toward a stronger pitch. Either double-check their name, their site's name, or something along those lines, or think of a way to bolster your pitch (i.e.: You remember a post they did that relates and go hunt it down to demonstrate that you have done your homework). We highly recommend you cultivate and listen to this little voice.

Send Three, Wait 30 Minutes, then Reread Your Email

In the case of automated outreach, we recommend sending only a few, waiting a standard amount of time, and then going back to the emails to double-check them. You may even get some early feedback that helps you to tighten up your engagement. Of course, you've already spent hours on the template.

It's tight, reads well, and you feel like it's going to incite some solid mentions and links. But you misspelled a name that spellcheck couldn't catch and in your hustle to get the email done you missed it. Or maybe some of your interview questions aren't as clear as you thought, and you end up with five people asking for clarification and 500 people putting the interview off until never. These are examples of conversion killers.

Pay special attention to the subject line, especially after sending off your first burst of 5 to 10 percent of your emails. Does it entice people to open by expressing the benefit to them or their readers? Does it have a misspelling? DOH!

While we've never gotten openly flamed, we have deserved it a time or two. Here are the mistakes we no longer make in content-based outreach for acquisition:

- Wrong name
- Wrong site name
- Subject lines that don't entice
- Misspellings in subject lines
- Poorly worded or confusing interview questions
- Too many interview questions
- Contacting sites that sell links with content-oriented outreach
- Cold outreach without preciprocation
- Not aligning link prospects with linkable assets
- Requesting homepage links from expert publishers
- Using the word "link"

HANDLING OUTREACH RESPONSES: IGNORES, ACCEPTS, DECLINES, AND COUNTERS

Once you've sent all your emails, it's time for the links, responses, and tweets to come rolling in . . . right? Well . . . we certainly hope so, but we never count on it, and we hope you don't either. This section will help you to prepare for what could happen after those emails go out. We hold that, broadly speaking, there are four possible ways for someone to respond to your email. They can:

- Ignore it
- Accept it and take action to mention your site
- Send an actual email declining your request, or
- Counter your request.

In this section we'll explore some tips for each possibility.

Ignores: If at First You Don't Succeed

You can try one more time—maybe your email got swept away under the deluge of daily emails this person gets. Try them again. But only one more time. Maybe two. Here are some tips:

- Always send a custom second email. Always. If you don't have the time to make your second request custom, then you shouldn't be sending it. Don't just resend your original request!
- Do include the original email text, though! Just make sure it's underneath the custom note you send.
- Mention any "big names" who have responded to your request so far. This helps demonstrate value.

- Maybe they're just busy, not ignoring you. Give them a few days to get back before sending something again.
- Consider looking for a different contact at that organization.
- If you STILL don't get anything back, take their name out of your contact rotation. From now on, the only time you should ever contact this person again is if they write to you first.

Accepts: WooHoo! Now What?

Congrats! You got the link, you got the tweet, you got the Facebook update, you got the cover story of *Time* magazine! Now what? There are a number of things you should be prepared to do.

- Say thank you. Emails are nice. Tweets are nice. Future links from you are nicest. Keep that fire going!
- Ask if they need content (assuming you have writers).
- Ask if you can interview their expert.
- Depending on click-throughs and traffic value, ask what other kinds of content would they be interested in sharing.
- Ask if they're interested in interviewing you (assuming you have a thought leader in your organization).
- Offer to make any personal introductions that you perceive could be useful to them.
- Follow/friend them if you're not already.

Declines: Wait, What? Why Not?

It happens. Sometimes people write you back to thank you for thinking of them but say they're not interested in sharing what you sent to them. The bare fact that they actually responded—even though it was in the negative—is a very positive and powerful thing. Here are some things you should do when you receive declines.

- Say thank you. And mean it.
- Put on your "objective scientist" pants and ask them, in as few words as possible, while expressing your boundless delight in their decision to respond, why they have declined your request.
- Learn what they would be willing to share in the future.
- Confirm their willingness to hear from you again ("When/if I create *x*, may I ping you again?").

Counters: Some People May Negotiate

In spaces in which publishers are highly aware of the value of a link, you're likely to encounter some counters to your emails, especially if you're going the request route and haven't adequately preciprocated your space. They may add a few hoops for you in order to earn your link. It's probably worth it, unless those hoops are money. Then you need to double-check your agenda and decide whether or not you want to be an organization that pays for links. But if those hoops are, say, a special discount for the site's readers, then let them know that you'll talk to the appropriate folks to decide whether or not you can move forward and offer discount in exchange for a link.

ACQUISITION TRACKING: KEEPING TABS ON YOUR EFFORTS

Depending on your specific goals for outreach, there are many things you can and should track. We created an outreach spreadsheet (linked from this chapter, in the tools section) that contains the following tabs. This is a good starting point for your brainstorm regarding what you will track:

- Targeted Host name/Link Page
- Contact's Name
- Email Address
- Date of 1st Contact
- Date of Follow-up
- Link Placed? Y/N
- URL of Placed Link
- Date Link Placed
- Linked URL
- Anchor Text Used
- Site Type
- Email Subject Line
- Opening Line
- Offer Made
- Growing the Relationship
- Twitter Address
- Notes

SUBMISSION ACQUISITION: COVERING YOUR BASES

While this chapter focuses on links that are earned via great content and relationship building, you've probably already brainstormed some link opportunity types that will require more one-touch, submission type of actions in order to earn them. These are likely to be opportunities like event aggregators, niche directories, PDF submission sites, etc. There's rarely a reason *not* to go for these opportunities. Just remember that they have a very low barrier to entry, meaning that just about any site can get them without having to earn all that trust we talk about building and leveraging in this chapter.

Submission acquisition is a grind, but you should do it anyway. Here is a preparedness checklist that will make it go faster for you:

- ❑ List of your qualified link prospects
- ❑ An email address for the person who is responsible for the link to your site
- ❑ Spreadsheet for recording logins/passwords per site
- ❑ Ideal anchor text and variations for each URL
- ❑ Description snippet prepared and variations thereof
- ❑ Ideal categories
- ❑ Physical address of company
- ❑ Credit card billing information (when applicable)

The more info you can gather ahead of time the faster this kind of work can be. Grit your teeth, grind it out, and get it done. And always err on the side of relevance to your target keywords, especially relevance to your target audience.

FIGURE 16–1. Submission Acquisition Checklist

LINK RELATIONSHIP MANAGEMENT TOOLS

There are several specialty tools designed to facilitate the growth of link relationships. We can't currently make a recommendation between them, but the most popular ones at publication are:

- BuzzStream
- Raven
- SearchReturn
- BuzzGain

FIGURE 16–2. BuzzStream Contact Info

Chapter 17

What a Link Request Might Look Like

A link request sent via email should include several elements. Collectively, these elements serve two key purposes. First, they let the person you are contacting know that without a doubt you took the time to actually look through his or her site, and second, make it as easy as possible for that person to make a decision whether or not to give your site a link.

12 ELEMENTS OF IRRESISTIBLE SUBMISSION REQUESTS

Email inboxes are busy (see Figure 17–1) and you need a way to make your email stand out from all the hundreds of others. Here are 12 elements your link requests should contain, followed by the logic behind them. Although these may seem obvious once you read the logic behind them, the overwhelming majority of link requests we receive do not contain them, so adopting these practices will set you apart from the competition for your target's attention. While in certain cases there are also other elements, for this chapter, we'll focus on the following 12.

1. *A subject line that follows any stated directions given on the site you want to link to yours.* On many sites with collections of links to other

PR Daily News Feed	47KB alan@ericward.com	◦ Storify for PR; First Lady wows DNC; Delivering bad news; 5 grammar lessons from NY
Agatha Alix	1KB hardinnn@urlwire.com	◦ 12c4
HARO	115KB Eric Ward	◦ [HARO] Wednesday Afternoon Queries "Nice to Meet You!" Edition
Darline	1KB mcdaniel@urlwire.com	◦ 6r9t6
Daria	1KB pena@urlwire.com	◦ dpu0mb
LaylaMarla	1KB gregoryt@urlwire.com	◦ e3dxo
Maribeth Kimberlie	1KB beasley@urlwire.com	◦ czt
Shayne Marcelle	1KB blankenship@urlwire.com	◦ ywxb
Ivory Danyell	1KB azar@urlwire.com	◦ vn9
St. Thomas Newsroom	37KB Lingua Publica	◦ [The Midweek] March Through the Arches Time-lapse Video
Appalachian Underwriters, Inc.	28KB shannon@thewardgroup.com	◦ Need Insurance for Waste Haulers?
Appalachian Underwriters, Inc.	28KB Wanda	◦ Need Insurance for Waste Haulers?
About.com Today	37KB eric@NETPOST.COM	◦ About Today: Falling in Love
Michelle Swayze: In Your Face Apparel	22KB editorrequest@urlwire.com	◦ BRIGHTEST SUPPORT POSSIBLE
Michelle Swayze: In Your Face Apparel	22KB eric@ericward.com	◦ BRIGHTEST SUPPORT POSSIBLE
Phone Systems Buyer	14KB ericz@ericward.com	◦ The Top Office Phone Systems for Your Business
Phone Systems Buyer	14KB pcmag@netpost.com	◦ The Top Office Phone Systems for Your Business
Charlie Sports	9KB eric@urlwire.com	◦ tues 500* mlb triple lock wins! thurs (6-0) 500* NFL Side & Total, 500* MLB triple lock
Wine.com	109KB mtrentha@netpost.com	◦ Grgich Napa Valley Cabernet & Chardonnay + 10% savings
The Daily Beast	31KB Eric Ward	◦ WATCH LIVE: Beast TV Special Coverage of the DNC
Ginny Grimsley	8KB eric@ericward.com	◦ Article: Bedroom Secrets from Nurse
White Paper Spotlight by Web Buyer's Guide	16KB pcmag@netpost.com	◦ Leveraging GRC Initiatives Towards Corporate Growth
Bioscience Technology	39KB BDURLWIRESRO@URLWIRE.C...	◦ Little Evidence of Health Benefits from Organic Foods
ChrisKanakis(sag-e)	4KB undisclosed-recipients;	◦ *-->WOW ChrisKanakis(sag-e) LEG Modeling!!??
Larry Angello: Metropak	22KB eric@ericward.com	◦ ooooo
Larry Angello: Metropak	22KB editorrequest@urlwire.com	◦ ooooo
ELMERCORY	1KB si@netpost.com	vl6
Belia Lakeesha	1KB ivybxzw@netpost.com	kq1ue7
GlennaRema	1KB sncalb@netpost.com	herz
LEISHA GAIL	1KB egviffy@netpost.com	b2wuy1
Lavona Milda	1KB knoejaqt@netpost.com	8pnpjz
AndreClaude	1KB cmirror@netpost.com	hpuv30
Terri Jacalyn	1KB uobhimself@netpost.com	tt3yy
HRWatch	24KB amatziabenartzi@netpost.com	Creating Friction-Free Relationships: Tools for Working with Anyone
Tech Insider	7KB Eric Ward	Is There a Hole in Your App Development Process? 3 Reasons to Use Data Masking
service@posterburner.com	16KB eric@ericward.com	◦ PosterBurner Order Confirmation
Charterhouse Leads	8KB cbfloamily@urlwire.com	◦ The Most Highly Recommended Point-Of-Sale Consumer Software Presentation In Th
Business Enhancement	4KB eric@ericward.com	◦ unbelievable prices on biz phone products
Support Paul Ryan	26KB inquiries@urlwire.com	◦ Paul Ryan vs. Joe Biden - It's Not Even Close
Site of the Day	7KB sotd@freelists.org	[sotd] West Nile Virus Running Wild [September 5, 2012]
Phil Sharkey: TK Cups-Sorgs	21KB editorrequest@urlwire.com	Make a statement
The Weather Channel Alerts	16KB undisclosed-recipients;	Your Pollen Alert for Santa Rosa Beach, FL
Newswatch	20KB tg1003658@onemain.com	Why Most PowerPoint Presentations Stink ... And How to Be Sure Yours Don't, Septem
TrainingIndustry.com	23KB eward@ericward.com	Training Industry Quarterly Fall 2012 – Now Online!
Fabulous-Furs	16KB lee@thewardgroup.com	Bring Out Your Inner Fashionista!
Building a Business Case from IT Business Edge	12KB eric@ericward.com	How to Quantify Projected Benefits of Your IT Investments
Mike Mansbach, Citrix	34KB amatziabenartzi@netpost.com	5 essential tips for getting a better ROI from webinars
1-800 CONTACTS	17KB melissatrentham@netpost.com	Limited time offer	Free Shipping on all orders
MobileCON™	11KB amatziabenartzi@netpost.com	Sign up for App-solutely Enterprise at MobileCON™ 2012!
The Weather Channel Alerts	13KB undisclosed-recipients;	Flood Warning for Santa Rosa Beach, FL
The Weather Channel Alerts	12KB undisclosed-recipients;	River Flood Warning for Santa Rosa Beach, FL
SEJ News	12KB SEJ-BEAT@LISTS.SEJ.ORG	[SEJ-BEAT]	Environmental News for September 5, 2012

FIGURE 17–1. An Email Inbox Is a Busy Place, and You Are Vying for Attention

sites (for example, some of the About.com guides), the editor in charge of link evaluation/selection often states that when asking for a link, you should follow specific directions. One of these directions is typically a special subject line, such as, "Request for editorial consideration."

If you have not taken the time to look at their site carefully, or even if you have, and you do not follow their stated link request directions, don't be surprised if you never hear from them and don't get the link. If the site gives exact instructions for submissions, then you have a bigger challenge. Do not put the words "link request" in the subject line, simply because there are probably about 100 million emails with that exact subject line or something similar hitting inboxes and getting deleted every day.

2. *The site owner's name.* It seems simple, but take the time to look through the site where you want the link, and find the site owner's name. Address this person by name immediately in your email. To begin an email with "Dear Webmaster" or "Site Owner" is to be deleted immediately. Can't find a name on the site? Look for a phone number. Call them. Yes, actually use the phone.

If you have a website with a personal URL in your name, and someone sends you a "Dear Webmaster" link, it will be immediately obvious to you that the sender has not been to your site even though their email indicates otherwise. If this person really had been to your site, your name would have been the first thing he or she would have seen. People might overlook the mistake but you'll increase your chances of getting your foot in the door if you take the time to address the site owner.

3. *Your name.* Again, it's just common courtesy. The person requesting a link is a human being and so are you. A first line like, "Hello, Mr. Ward, my name is Bill Thompson," tells Mr. Ward that Bill looked at his site and respects basic human conversational etiquette. It also shows Mr. Ward that you didn't send that same email to 4,000 other people, unless by some bizarre coincidence their names were all Mr. Ward.

4. *The URL of their site.* Using wording such as, "I see that on your site you have the following content at the below URL" allows you to use a template approach but also shows the site owner you know their name, site, and a specific URL. You obviously are not lying to them or spamming them.

   Don't show fake sincerity or imply friendship when in fact you've never met. Be professional, courteous, and to the point. People really get turned off by email from strangers who act like their buddies.

5. *Your site's name and the URL you are hoping they will link to.* For example, "I am contacting you about my site, called [SiteName], which is located at [URL]."

6. *The exact URL on their site where you think the link is a fit.* "With regard to your page located at http://www.[page URL]." This is especially helpful for those people who maintain large sites with hundreds or thousands of pages. Help them to help you.

7. *A short paragraph that describes your site.* Do not oversell your site or give them 76 reasons why they should link to it. If they link to it, it won't be your email that convinced them. It will be because they looked at your site and determined whether or not it's link-worthy to them based on their criteria.

8. *The exact URL from your site you want them to link to.* "Since I have a splash page that has some Flash elements, you may prefer to use this URL for linking: http://www. SiteName.com/noflash.html."

9. *A valid email address and response to any requests made to that address.* "If you would like to contact me about this, please feel free to reach me at my personal email address below." (List your email address.)

10. *Your phone number.* "Or, if you prefer, you can also call me at this phone number . . ."

And, if you are seeking a link from a site where a return link is required (I don't, but many do), also include:

11. *Confirmation that you have added a link to their site.*

12. *The URL on your site where they can see the link to their site.*

What your email doesn't say is just as important.

Any webmaster, editor, curator, or site manager who receives the email outlined in Figure 17–2 can tell immediately several crucial things about this link request:

To:

From: You@yourdomain.com

Subject: Site submission

Dear [Site Owner Name],

I am contacting you regarding your [full title of the site, not URL] site at [URL].

I'm working with [URL] to announce and link a new section on their site called [title of the site you want the link for].

Per the link request instructions on your site, I would like to request a link to our homepage in your Links to [website descriptor] Websites section located at [URL].

Please feel free to let me know if the above provides you with the information you need to review and consider our site for linking. I can be reached via email at you@yourdomain.com, or, if you'd like to talk about this by phone, my direct number is (123) 456-7890.

Best wishes,

Your Name

FIGURE 17–2. Sample of What a Full Link-Request Email Might Look Like

- It was sent by someone who took the time to actually look at the site. How else could they call it by name?
- It was sent by someone who took the time to find out who runs the site.
- It was sent by someone who reviewed the site for appropriateness. How else would they have known the site had a "links" area related to their own content?
- It was sent by someone who followed the site editor's link request instructions.
- It was sent by someone who couldn't have sent that same email to 25,000 people.
- It was sent by someone who respected the website owner's time by making it easy for him or her to know just what URL they wanted linked.
- It was sent by someone who looked at more than just the prospect domain's homepage.
- It was sent by someone who was not afraid to put a phone number in the email; spammers don't do that.

There are many more subtle points to this exercise illustrated in Figure 17–2, and many additional things you might need or have to include, but these are not right for every scenario, so let's keep things as simple as possible for now. This particular letter was designed for a link builder working on behalf of a site owner; if you were the site owner yourself you would delete the sentence beginning "I'm working with" and edit the rest of the letter accordingly.

The bottom line is that by recognizing the individuals on the receiving end of your link requests, you immediately move out of the spam realm in their minds. When most folks receive link letters, they look for telltale signs that they were not singled out individually. If they spot an obvious bulk link seeker, they usually delete it immediately.

This means you cannot automate this process and it means you have to create and send each link request one at a time. As you should. Sometimes each site takes an entire three clicks and two minutes. Big deal. This is a lifelong link you're seeking.

Chapter 18

Putting the Pieces Together
Link-Building Campaign Templates

I t's always helpful to have some examples of link-building campaigns when designing your own. These are some general templates we've found useful in our work. If you're ready to get started right away, you may have skipped directly to this section. That's fine—just note that the underlying concepts are more important in campaign design than the templates, but the templates are great for seeing where the concepts can take you.

THE ULTIMATE RESOURCE AGGREGATION PIECE

In the ultimate resource aggregation piece, you're creating a massive list, or roundup, of an informational resource that your market finds useful. Ideally, you're also recontextualizing it in some way that adds more value than if a reader found one of the individual pieces alone. This can be in the form of a process walkthrough, or some other framework that your market will find useful.

Remember, you're ideally selecting your resources for this piece from among the link targets in your keyword space.

Resource Aggregation Examples

Here are some additional examples of resource aggregations you can check out on the web. Note that each one has its own framework or context for the resources that introduces them and makes them more accessible.

FIGURE 18–1. An Example of Link Aggregation Content

- 18 Must-Follow Link-Building Experts on Twitter: http://www.huomah.com/Internet-Marketing/Link-Building/18-Must-Follow-Link-Building-Experts-on-Twitter.html
- 35 Expert-Recommended Link Building Tools: http://ontolo.com/blog/b-35-expert-recommended-link-building-tools.html
- The reasonable surfer; makes for unreasonable thinkers (phenomenal example of resource aggregation with Explanation and Interpretation as a value add)
- Life or Debt? 41 Financial Calculators for Major Life Decisions

Resource Types

There are a number of resource types you can and should consider aggregating. These include, but are not limited to the following:

- How-tos and guides
- Videos
- Top (your industry) Twitter users

FIGURE 18–2. Example of a Tool Aggregation Piece That Will Attract Links

- Blogs
- PDFs
- Free tools/paid tools
- Podcasts
- Classes
- All the "Top #" lists for a topic (top 10, top 100, etc.)

People, Work Hours, and Cash Required

This one is all about applying your talent and work hours. What's nice about the resource aggregation piece is that it's fairly fast if you're already an expert in a space, and it's a fantastic "crash course" to the top thinkers and publishers if you're new. Ideally these are not pieces you dash off, but rather spend time looking for new and more useful ways to organize the information. What will make your collection of links more useful than others? Can you somehow come up with a score for each link or a rating? Do you have personal information you can add to each resource mention? Can you present the links within the framework of a process, or within some other framework recognizable in your industry?

This can take someone who's an old hand in a space about a day to research, categorize, find new patterns, and publish. Someone who's new to a space could/should spend two or more days, ideally.

Link Prospect Sources

Ideally the resources you link to in the first place are your link prospects. It is probable that the expert publishers in your space will take interest in a new configuration of previously existing resources.

Here's where your title and pitch come into play! Further prospects include sites and pages linking to the same resources *you* linked to.

Finally, you can try some of these queries to turn up some new prospects for you:

- **[MDFK] blogs** – You'll want to let your industry's bloggers know about you, even if they're not in the resource.
- **"[MDFK] news"**
- **[MDKW] community** – Some forum owners might be interested in sharing your resource, or give you permission to share it within their communities.
- **[MDKW] roundup**
- **"useful [MDKW] links"**

Tips and Helpful Hints

Resource-list inclusion makes a wonderful introduction to experts in your market and is a great way to start off a campaign if you're completely new to a keyword space. To up your chances of getting links from this kind of piece, include resources from writers who consistently create roundups of the space. If they're writing about the space consistently anyway, they're more likely to link to you.

We've created badges for bloggers in our resource lists before, but found that these badges ended up making the linked-to pages on our clients' sites look spammy. We suspect this is because they were site wides.

Numbers—as in the number of resources—can be an effective way to communicate the size and enormity of your resource list. There are some SEOs who believe that numbers and lists are losing their effectiveness. We suspect that this could be true in some spaces, and especially if the resources are not organized in a new, interesting, and more useful way.

Figure 18–3 on page 123 is an example of an outreach email template for your next "Ultimate Resource Roundup." Add to it and subtract from it as you see fit!

Subject line: You're in [Title of Resource Roundup]! Yay! ;)

Just a quick note to let you know that we included you in [Title of Resource Roundup]

http://www.hostname.com/YourResourceRoundup

We linked to: http://www.theirsite.com/theirresource

Will you help us spread the word about your inclusion in the roundup?

What really sets our roundup apart is that it [customize your message].

Also, if you're a member of [NicheSocialNewsSite.com], will you consider voting for this post?

http://NicheSocialNewsSite.com/YourResourceRoundup

Thank you!

Your Name

FIGURE 18–3. Sample Outreach Template for the Ultimate Resource Roundup

THE GROUP INTERVIEW/SURVEY OF EXPERTS AND OTHER MARKET PARTICIPANTS

We've found that interviewing the expert publishers in a space—that is, the frequent writers, contributors and active participants within a given industry, hobby, or other "thought space"—is an excellent way to build links, create great content, as well as to connect you more powerfully with your market. We've engaged expert/hobbyist forums in this way as well, to fantastic result.

Examples of Group Interviews and Expert Surveys

Here are some examples of group interviews and expert surveys. Note that there superficially appears to be a relationship between the quality of the graphics and overall presentation and links. Any time you can create pleasing presentations for your data, your link traction will improve.

- Search Engine Ranking Factors
- Interview: 12 Top Online Entrepreneurs Share How Hard They Work
- 21 Link Builders Share Advanced Link-Building Queries
- 30 Link Builders Discuss Backlink Analysis For Campaign Design—Part 1
- ToolCrib.com's Ultimate Guide to the Top Ten Most Dangerous Woodworking Power Tools

QUESTION DESIGN: WARNING . . . YOU GET WHAT YOU ASK FOR

On a number of occasions we've asked way too many questions of our experts. In one instance we sought to publish a single article, asked 10 questions of 30 experts and got back 30,000 words (enough for 30+ articles).

We've never asked too few questions. In fact, here's a great example of a group interview article with only one question: "(44 Experts Discuss) Social Media Strategy Before Tactics." However, if you ask your questions in a way that forces your experts to explicitly quantify their answers (with numbers, for example) you can create this kind of a result: Link Value Factors. Wow! What a beauty! In this piece the survey creator wasn't overly concerned with too much input—because the answers got quantified and graphed it helped reliability of data to have more input! Also, when possible, focus on hot, potentially even controversial, topics. This will help you to get some interest from others in your space.

People, Work Hours, and Cash Required

When it comes to group surveys, the bigger, the better, usually. Ideally you're gathering enough input, thought, and wisdom that you can create multiple pieces. It's tough to put numbers on this, but something like "(44 Experts Discuss) Social Media Strategy Before Tactics" could probably take around a day to aggregate and publish. Something like "Interview: 12 Top Online Entrepreneurs Share How Hard They Work" probably didn't take forever, either.

Link Prospect Sources

In this case, your best prospects are the participants themselves. In markets where we've gone in cold, we've found about a 20-percent rate of links and mentions from participants. In every case, we've found that the number of links is at least double the number of participants.

Tips and Helpful Hints

Ask people if they will participate in your group interview/expert survey *as* you're asking them to mention or link to something else. Also, as in the resource roundup described above, make sure to include roundup publishers in your group of experts. They are most likely to link! See Figure 18–4.

Subject line 1: May I Interview You? and Potential Article for a Roundup

Subject line 2: Group Interview—You In?

Hello!

I have two requests for you—1) to add your voice to a group [Subject Matter] interview I'll be publishing and promoting next month and 2) to consider a recent piece I wrote for a mention in one of your upcoming roundups!

To be included in the interview I will need your answers by [date]! If appropriate, feel free to provide links to any blog posts you've done that answer questions more fully!

1. What's your "[Subject Matter] story?" In other words, how and why did you get started in [Subject Matter]?

2. What [Subject Matter] skills were the hardest for you to learn and why?

3. Have you ever taken [Subject Matter] too far or failed spectacularly in some way? How so?

4. What resources (blogs, books, websites) would you recommend to someone who's new to the [Subject Matter] arena?

5. What question did I leave off/what message would you really like to get out there?

6. Who else should I interview?

>> And here's the article I hope you'll consider for a roundup:
[article title] [article URL]

Or will you give us a tweet? [article title] http://bit.ly/articleurl

Or just a vote on NicheSocialNewsSite.com? :D
http://NicheSocialNewsSite.com/titleofthepiece/
[Pitch the value of your piece]

Thanks for your consideration and I look forward to getting your answers!

[Your Name]

FIGURE 18–4. Sample Outreach Template for the Expert Interview/Survey Piece

YOUR OWN HIGH-QUALITY, LEAD-GENERATING, BRAND-BUILDING CONTENT

Ideally, by the time you get around to pushing your own content on others for link consideration you have amply warmed up your link prospects by promoting them, helping them spread their message, and demonstrating that you both care about the audience and the industry as a whole. By engaging your link prospects in this manner, you have sown the seeds of trust. They are now more likely to consider mentioning work you have done—work that does not directly promote them in some way. Especially if it's great content.

Examples of High-Quality, Lead-Generating, Brand-Building Content

Ideally your content pushes your industry's thought forward, delivers relevant traffic, confers a bit of reputation on your brand by association (from where you earn mention and links, or, if you publish it offsite, from the publisher's brand), and even generates business leads. That's quite a tall order, right? Isn't this supposed to be a book about link building? Well, we believe that this sort of content is the highest form of link building, in that it satisfies so many different objectives simultaneously. It's what we strive for in our own marketing, and it's what we urge our clients, prospects, and the market as a whole to work toward. No, it's not easy, and it takes a lot of attempts before you start really getting it right. Here are some examples of content that does it all right (forgive our hubris in mentioning some of our content here—note that it should also help you in the content-creation phase):

- Link Building with Content: How to Attract Links and Leads
- 101 Ways to Build Link Popularity
- How to Research, Create, and Distribute Highly Linkable Content
- The Link Prospector

People, Work Hours, and Cash Required

Creating this kind of content—whether it's a tool, article, video, or whatever—requires significant investments of time. There's no easy way around this one! At some point you have to put your position or your organization's position out there in a format that's going to help you achieve multiple business goals simultaneously.

Notes and Tips

To make your content more linkable and reputable, you may have to go to the experts in your organization, and lean on them to share their time and expertise (the same way you initially went to the expert publishers in your space). For our own marketing, we've found that free tools and process-oriented spreadsheets are highly linkable, and demonstrate our capacity for deriving value from link-prospect data. Remember that you have to *give* to your industry in order to *receive* the links and leads!

It's vital to not always be the platform and the connector. Though this does serve to build links, you also have to be an originator. This is what builds the leads. Prospects want to see your original thought, not just that you can recognize and cultivate great thought in others!

Dear [Contact Name],

I'm writing today to introduce: http://citationlabs.com/36-broken-link-building-resources/.

This URL collection walks motivated readers through the methods and processes of large-scale, research-intensive broken-link building.

We include a number of your writings and resources there. In addition, we promote [your tools] as good data-gathering alternatives for link builders without crawler/scraper technology.

My request to you is that you check out our new guide and mention it if you find it noteworthy.

Thank you for your consideration!

Best,

[Your Name]

FIGURE 18–5. Sample Outreach for High-Quality, Lead-Generating, Brand-Building Content

EXPERT ENGAGEMENT: THE "WRITING ASSIGNMENT"

In creating a writing assignment or prompt for your expert publishers, you first come up with an intriguing concept or question—perhaps one left over from your interview questions. Then you answer this question yourself on your site and implore your visitors to do the same. The goal is to make it something that others would genuinely have the urge to write about in their next blogging session. Then you promote the heck out of your question. Furthermore, as part of the promotion, make sure that contributors know you'll be linking to their answers.

Some Examples of Expert Engagement Writing Assignments

Here are a few samples of expert engagement writing assignments we've found "in the wild."

- A letter to myself
- Create Your Own "Bloggers to Watch" List and Tell Us About It Here
- ToolCrib.com's Guide to Your 31 Most Influential Woodworkers (a hybrid writing assignment/expert survey)

People, Work Hours, and Cash Required

This method is fairly simple to execute, though it will require maintenance as you correspond with experts and add their contributions to your site. Also, it's not likely to work as well if you're entering a space "cold." This method will be much more effective when done after building relationships in your space with the expert publishers and other contributors.

Notes and Tips

There are a number of ways you can spin this approach to link building. If you've done a massive survey, you could give away your data and ask others for their interpretations. You could also combine this effort with your group interview and simply ask people to answer your questions on their site. Then your job as the editor/curator will be to collect and aggregate the most interesting and important data as you see it.

We've only done this technique once, after a group expert interview piece we created for a client got mentioned in Time.com. We took the "distributed group interview" approach and asked a large number of experts to weigh in. We also told them that we'd be sending their answers to our contact at Time.com, which we did. We did *not* ask them to link to the original, though many of them did. See Figure 18–6.

FREE PRODUCTS AND SERVICES: CONTESTS, DONATIONS, AND GIVEAWAYS

This is about the closest we get to buying links in this book. And, yeah, it's pretty close. It happens on calls with clients and prospects, especially those seeking our link prospect data and not our agency services; they have no time or desire to contribute great content

Subject line: Share Your Hard-Earned [Subject Matter] Lessons with Time.com!

Hello!

I'm a new [Subject Matter] blogger, so when I emailed interview questions to famous [Subject Matter] bloggers like [expert], [expert], and [expert] I got pretty nervous. After all, I only started blogging a few months ago. Why would these pros answer my questions?

Well, I'm glad I faced my fears and emailed them because they *did* answer my interview questions, and after I published their answers ([link to client site where story appeared]), Time.com picked up the story!

I know there are more than just their lessons out there. And I know that you must have some of them!

Here's how to add your wisdom to the group interview, and get a shot at a mention in Time.com!

1. Answer the questions below and post them to your blog
2. Tweet @[client] and email [your address] to let us know they're up
3. Add a link to your answers in the comment section of our group interview in order to share it with visitors from Time.com!
4. I will email Time.com on April 15, send a complete list of who else responded, and ask them to check out our group interview again!

We had [##] responses to our original interview. To get Time's attention again, I'd really like to add at least 100 more! Here are your interview questions:

1. What's your "[Subject Matter] story?" In other words, how and why did you become a [Subject Matter] expert?
2. What, if anything, tempts you to do [Subject Matter] poorly, and how do you resist?
3. What [Subject Matter] habits were the hardest for you to adopt and why?
4. Have you ever taken [Subject Matter] too far? How so?
5. What resources (blogs, books, websites) would you recommend to someone who's new to [Subject Matter]?

Thank you for your consideration, and I look forward to writing to Time.com with your contribution!

FIGURE 18–6. Sample Outreach for the Writing Assignment

to their space in exchange for links. Furthermore, there's often an SEO-driven mentality to acquire links with some sort of immediate and direct value exchange. To protect the innocent, we're not going to point out sites accepting donations in exchange for links. Instead, we'll focus on the more fun contests we've seen that leverage giveaways!

Some Examples

- Andy Beal's SEM Scholarship
- Design My New Business Card & Win Free Business Cards FOR LIFE

Chapter 19

Building Links and Expertise with Guest Post Placement Campaigns

A guest post is an article, written by you, placed on someone else's site. PR professionals call this a "bylined article." A guest post campaign occurs when you increase the scale of the processes required for a single placement of a guest post. There are agencies out there doing 800+ guest post placements a month.

KNOW YOUR AUDIENCE'S NAME

It's rare to talk with an SEO link builder who's targeting a specific audience—most have specific keywords in mind that they want to rank for. To gauge the viability of a guest placement campaign you must first translate these keywords into a target audience. Let's say your client wants to rank for web hosting and they specialize in hosting for small, online business owners.

BRAINSTORM MORE TARGET AUDIENCES

Starting from their target of "small online business owners" you can parse out some potential audiences. This is done primarily by "thinking like a directory" and determining what categories a resource for "small online business owners" could fit into. It's well worth visiting a directory to help the brainstorming process.

For example:

- Small business
- Online business
- Ecommerce
- Web design

Also, take a pass at your audience keywords with the Ubersuggest tool mentioned on page 71. Once you have your audience keywords figured out, it's time to run a quick viability check.

QUICK VIABILITY CHECK—"[TARGET AUDIENCE]" + INTITLE: "WRITE FOR US"

Take your target audiences and combine them with the command intitle:"write for us". Pages that have "write for us" in the title tag indicate a demand for content. Assuming you have effectively named your target audience, the quantity of results generated with this query along with the number of viable prospects in the top 10 to 20 results will give you a sense of whether a guest placement campaign is viable and at what scale.

If you see 2 to 300 results for each query, with 3 to 5 definite opportunities in the top 10, you can reasonably estimate 10 guest-post placements per query run (based on

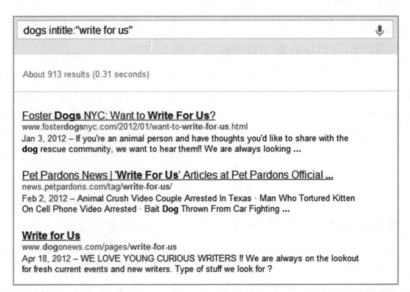

FIGURE 19–1. The Very Presence of Write for Us Pages Indicates that the Keyword Used Will Deliver Prospects—and Could Be Useful in Prospecting for Other Tactics

20 percent conversion). This quick test will let you know whether you need to really conduct a full inventory, or if you need to go back and think a bit further about your target audience.

You may find that there isn't significant volume and quality of opportunities for SERP impact at all, or recognize that you need to supplement with other higher-volume opportunity types.

IDENTIFY THE VOLUME OF PLACEMENT/POSTING OPPORTUNITIES

If you're seeing strong signs of content demand you can start to expand your querying into a full-blown inventory—or at least set up the queries for someone else to do the prospecting for you.

Here is an excellent rundown of queries for thoroughly prospecting for guest publication opportunities. Remember to keep your eyes peeled for the footprints of prolific guest posters in your vertical—they will lead you to other opportunities. If you find guest posters with footprints across hundreds of sites, then set those aside for high-volume, low-value placement opportunities. They're out there, and you can definitely get to larger scale with them.

By measuring the volume of opportunity you will know how many writers you'll need to cover all the available opportunities.

GAUGE THE QUALITY OF PLACEMENT OPPORTUNITIES

Quantity isn't all you need to look at, especially if you have your eyes on branding and reach. Here are some thoughts on gauging the value of a guest-posting opportunity:

- Copy and paste the title of a two-week-old article and search for it in quotes. Where does it appear? Are there scrapers, is the title in Twitter, does the site syndicate their RSS feed, etc.? This will give you a bit of insight into how wide the reach is for a given publication.
- Check how many tweets, shares, and +1s articles get on a site—this will show you the social reach that the publication has developed.
- Check the quality and quantity of comments to get a sense of the community surrounding the site.
- Does the publisher aggressively link from within the article to their own pages? Check for it—it's fairly common and could affect the SERP impact of your efforts.
- Scan their backlinks—are any recognizable sites linking in? This will give you a sense of who's reading and linking to the publisher.

- Are guest posters using exact match anchors or brand names? This can be an indicator of site policies.
- Do they require/request an ongoing content commitment? This can indicate a strong editorial hand, which usually means a higher-quality publication.

In investigating these items, you will get a sense of the characteristics your content will need to have to make it "placeable."

QUANTIFY THE LEVEL OF EXPERTISE IN EXISTING GUEST-PUBLISHED CONTENT

Now that you have your targets, it's time to figure out what level of subject matter expertise you'll need to meet your audience's information needs. Find out how readily available subject matter expertise is—are there forums, books, PDFs, etc., that you can use for research? Often when there's strong content demand, as exhibited by the presence of "write for us" pages, there's a ready availability of prepackaged expertise you can research and cite. If you're planning to "go big," it's also worth investigating how much or how little tip-based content exists. Note—you can use your audience keywords in your tip research, as well.

GENTLY CROSS-EXAMINE THE CLIENT BEFORE SIGNING THAT CONTRACT

Guest placements certainly build links, and that's often what gets SEOs interested in the first place. However, if you're publishing on the right sites, with the right content, you can begin establishing expertise within a given category. To really deliver for your client on this expertise building you'll have to get access to the client organization's subject-matter experts and get buy-in and sign-off. Here are some questions to ask before you get that contract with a new client signed.

- Is perceived brand expertise really a factor in the purchase decision?
- How involved can the client be in content ideation?
- Are there experts available for interviews?
- Does the client have published expertise (tools, PDFs, presentations, videos) that's suitable for promoting within guest placements?
- Is there unique data available relative to the client's market (that can be published)?
- Who has to approve content in the client's organization?
- How active is the client in social media channels, and do they intend to increase this activity?

- Can you get an @client.com email address (in under three months)?
- Whose name will be on the placements?
- Are there any do-not-contact publishers operating in your prospective client's MDKW space?

If it seems that the client is unable or unwilling to demonstrate expertise and build credibility, then guest placements (especially at high- and mid-quality publishers) are probably not a great direction and may not be suitable for inclusion in the overall link-building campaign design. If the client can see the value—the publicity, branding, and reach—of guest placements and is eager to share their expertise with the market, then you should see fantastic results.

Going big in guest posting requires careful planning at every stage, from viability analysis and prospect discovery on down to effective content design. Many sites offer guest blog posting tips and advice.

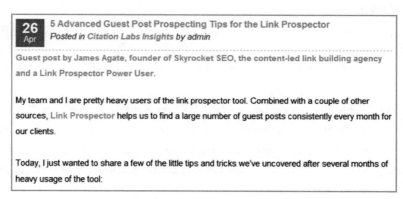

FIGURE 19–2. Guest Posting Tips

Note: This is outreach advice for campaigns in which all the content is written prior to placement. Some guest posters get content ideas approved by the publisher prior to actually writing. Getting publisher buy-in is fantastic and is much faster at the outreach stage. However, it slows the overall process and isn't advisable at larger scale, especially when client approval of content is required.

TRACKING THE OUTREACH PHASE'S "MOVING PARTS"

Outreach has many "moving parts" and a great deal to track in order to remain effective, efficient, and protective of the brand. Before digging into specific advice, here are several core elements to track in your campaign (these items also happen to make good columns for a spreadsheet).

Outreach Tracking Sheet 1

1. *List of outreach prospects*: At the beginning of any campaign, I prospect and project on 10-percent conversions, but usually get around 30 percent. If you have 10 posts, expect to need 100 different guest placement prospects.

2. *Specific niche focus*: Vital so that you can be sure you're pitching the right "flavor" of article to the appropriate blogger within a topic area (e.g., while email and SEO are two marketing methods, you shouldn't pitch your email marketing tips article to the SEO blog).

3. *Prospect contact information and/or contact URL*

4. *Anchor text/promotional link target*

5. *Notes*: Any tips or guidance to help your outreacher when they're neck-deep in the inbox and convoluted spreadsheet you sent them

Content Details Sheet 2

1. *List of completed content titles*. This is your master list of guest content inventory. This is what you're selling with your outreach emails.

2. *Specific niche focus of piece*. This will help you pitch the right titles to the right publishers.

3. *Content "status" for individual articles*. Use terms such as "written," "in consideration," "pending," and "placed" to track content status. *Written* needs promotion; *in consideration* means a publisher expressed interest and has it in their inbox; *pending* means the publisher said yes but hasn't published; and *placed* means it's live on their site.

4. *Domain of prospective publisher*. Replace with final published URL.

5. *Date of initial contact*. Use this to track to which sites you have already outreached.

OUTREACH: WHAT'S TEMPLATABLE, WHAT'S NOT

There are continual template/no template debates that go on in link outreach. Our experience is the more work you do in targeted prospecting and content design, the more templates you can use in your outreach. That's because you've done your homework and lined up the needs of your publishers with what you're pitching. This ensures obvious benefit to the publisher.

Using a "templating" approach can be as simple as using a single notepad application window and making alterations there or as complex as a merge macro in a word processing application.

Not Templatable

Here's what will need to be unique in every email you send:

1. *Establish initial rapport in the first sentence.* Don't overdo it though—they are publishers and very busy. Plus you're offering them free content. It's not like you're begging for a link or anything. Primarily, you're establishing how you identify with the target audience. For example, "I'm a busy mom of multiples who somehow finds time for freelance writing!"

2. *Prove you read their guest submission requirements.* Assuming guest publishing requirements exist—and about 20 percent of the time, they do—poke around and make sure what you're sending in fits.

3. *Two to three titles you're pitching.* Keep this number small. You don't want to give the sense that your email is part of a large, well-oiled campaign. Also, having fewer choices can make for a speedier response time.

4. *Benefits of pitched pieces to publisher's audience.* Usually the title of the piece needs to make the benefit clear, however, it never hurts to explain a bit about who the article helps and how it helps them.

Templatable

These are things you can reuse quite a bit. It's OK if you find yourself altering core aspects of templates as you go along for clarity, readability, and believability. Also, omit needless words.

1. *Who you are, who you're with, why you're writing.* Keep it cordial, brief, and easily alterable (this is your first sentence, which you will tailor per-site).

2. *Relevant accolades that could help them say yes more quickly.* Are you or is your writer or brand known for anything laudable? Mention it!

3. *Two or three most notable prior publications.* This helps demonstrate that you or your alias has content that others consider publishable. Also, publishers can read your previous work.

4. *Numbers of tweets, shares, +s, and links received by your guest publications.* This can be a deal-sealer if you can throw around some high numbers.

5. *How you will promote it once the post is up (tweet, share, link to it, email newsletter, etc.).*

6. *Your eagerness to make any changes they require.* Demonstrate that you're willing to work with them and make sure your content is a good fit for their audience.

P.S. The Piggyback Pitch

You've done all that prospecting, and you may as well piggyback another request or two into your outreach. Here are a few thoughts on an "Oh, and by the way" section of your outreach emails.

1. *New, high-utility content you're promoting for their roundups, for their Twitter followers, etc.*: Pitch your infographics, widgets, videos, new articles, etc.
2. *Ask if they accept items for contests/giveaways*: Many sites conduct giveaways to their readers. Do you have anything to offer?
3. *Ask if they will answer interview/survey questions.*

OUTREACH EXECUTION ADVICE

The best advice we can give you on outreach execution is to just dive in there and do it. It's the best way to learn.

1. *Send 10 to 20 emails and wait one or two days.* It takes a while for publishers to respond. Plus you're pitching unique content and don't want to overpromise a piece.
2. *Pitch titles, don't send or pitch pieces as complete.* Give the publishers the sense that you're writing pieces "on the fly." This will help reduce suspicion that you're pitching already-published content.
3. *Have "placed" folders on your hard drive so you don't double publish.* Oops! You sent two people the same content and they both published it? Doh! When a piece gets placed, move it or delete it so you never, ever attach it to another email and send it.
4. *Your spreadsheet doubles as a reporting sheet and prospect approval sheet.* Use your spreadsheet for project management, client reporting, and input. Centralize!
5. *Published-piece tracking and contact information helps you build a master sheet for repurposing down the road.* One of the biggest values you're building for your organization is a list of sites you can go back to with new content that supports new initiatives (and targets new keywords). Guest posts work great as off-site satellites promoting a flagship piece of content on your site.

Chapter 20

Broken Link-Building Campaigns

Broken link building is one of only a handful of highly-scalable AND white hat link building tactics. With this tactic you check your target website's outbound links to see if they're still up. If your target site links to a competitor's information page that's dead you then email the target site and suggest they link to you instead. As Russ Jones, CTO of Virante describes broken link building: "the success of the campaign is directly proportional to how much good you do for the web."

The process described in this chapter is not elegant, but it does help you cover a lot of ground—you can find and analyze thousands of resources and root out the dead pages and sites quite quickly. It is possible to build more than 40 links a month with this method while selling BLB prospecting as a service to others. As we have said before, link rot is your friend. Here's the process and the tools that we use and recommend.

SEARCH FOR 10 TO 100S OF LINKS PAGES

You guessed it—use your link prospector for this, and prospecting phrases that categorically represent the topic area you're promoting and plug those right into the tool. If you don't use the link prospector, you could try the prospecting queries mentioned here, and tildes, lots of tildes!

What you're looking for are curated links pages where your content could fit—with light scrutiny—whether you found a broken link or not. This of course presupposes you're promoting good quality, long-form content for which there are hundreds of "curators." If you search, and each of the top 10 pages are good prospects, then you're in a good space for this effort.

SEOs used to go through hundreds of pages and pick only those we thought had the highest relevance. Now we rarely spend much time "qualifying" links pages. We rely on our tools and common sense and just pass a big ol' batch of links pages right on over to—the next step.

SCRAPE OUTBOUND LINKS FROM THE PAGES

Next, using an outbound link scraper (one of the four tools in our scraper suite), scrape the outbound links from the batch of links pages you've found.

Recently, from a batch of 427 links pages we extracted 12,635 resource URLs. Were each of the links and resources pages perfectly relevant to the subject matter? They were close enough. We needed to cover lots of ground!

FIGURE 20-1. Outbound Link Scraper

CHECK THE STATUS OF EACH OUTBOUND LINK

Once extracting outbound links from the resource pages, it's time to check status. And, yup, we've got a tool for that in the scraper suite—the URL Status Checker. This tool checks and reports on the status of each URL, just as the name suggests. The tool does split large sets up into batches of 1,000. This means the 12,000-plus-URL project will be in 12 separate comma-separated value documents (CSVs). Yes, that's a pain, but that's the row you've chosen to hoe here so put your back into it. Merge the CSVs from this tool and sort them to isolate the dead and nonresponding pages from your set. This obviously can take some time.

And then . . .

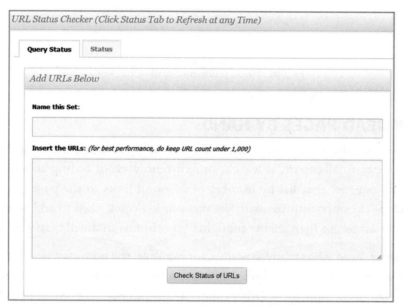

FIGURE 20–2. URL Status Checker

RECHECK THE STATUS OF EACH DEAD LINK FOR FINAL VERIFICATION

Recheck, because the tool's not 100 percent accurate, and it's heartbreaking further on in the process to think a site with 30,000 unique linking domains is dead when really it's just responding slowly. So recheck everything that the tool reports dead. Some people, whom we'll refrain from naming, check three times when feeling especially obsessive.

GATHER METRICS FOR THE DEAD/UNRESPONSIVE PAGES

We use Majestic SEO's bulk backlink checker for learning which dead URLs have the most linking domains, though they limit you to checking only 300 rows at a time. Simply copy and paste in 300 of your dead URLs, sort by the number of inbound linking domains, and you'll have a good idea of where to start your deeper investigations.

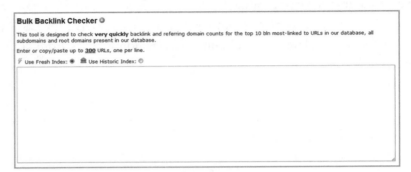

FIGURE 20–3. Bulk Backlink Checker

REVIEW DEAD PAGES BY HAND

Here's where the intuition starts, and the slow combing through URLs. And yes, this is where automation falls apart, at least at our current levels of coding and expertise. So, first things first, sort that list by number of inbound links to the page. This will give you a sense of the opportunities with the most links. You'll need to add some columns to your spreadsheet, so here are my thoughts on columns that will help your reviewing.

- *How is it "dead"?* For many .gov sites, for example, the non-www doesn't redirect to the www subdomain. And yet they sometimes have hundreds of linking domains pointed to the non-www. Other times the site is a parked domain now. Still other times it's just plain gone. All of this information is important for further on when you're writing your outreach emails.
- *Topic.* What is this dead page about, according to Archive.org? Does the site or page actually have anything to do with the site I'm promoting? I use Majestic SEO at this point also to check out anchor text as that gives a good clue if Archive.org doesn't have info.
- *How big is the opportunity?* Is the whole site dead? Just one section? Just one page? All this needs to be recorded so you can figure out how to best pull backlinks for the opportunity.
- *What are you promoting?* Is this a one-to-one replacement opportunity? (These are the best, whether you write it as you find it dead or already have something written.) Is it a fix suggestion and similar-resource link request?

Be sure to save any and all dead sites you find with 100 or more links—even if you can't use them now. You can always come back later or possibly come up with an angle down the road.

PULL AND QUALIFY DEAD BACKLINKS

With our metrics tool you can also pull backlinks for the dead links you'd like to pursue. Ah, but we wish we could tell you it was as easy as taking all the links and heading over to the contact finder (one of the tools in our scraper suite). Nope—you've got to scrub this data or you'll end up wasting your time.

First and foremost, do not get excited about apparently large lists of opportunities. It's quite common to start with 16,000 unique linking domains and boil those down to 50 actual opportunities for outreach. So don't tell clients how many ops you have for them until you've done your distilling—you will end up profoundly overselling what you have.

You can use Citation Labs' metrics suite for Linkscape data if you like and input each URL you'd like backlinks for. You then designate how many backlinks you want us to pull and pay us per backlink (one backlink—one row in a spreadsheet). I like to use Majestic SEO for this, too as they seem quite a bit fresher and more comprehensive. That said, Majestic SEO's comprehensiveness comes with a great deal more "scrubbing" required. Whether you use Linkscape data sourced through our metrics suite or Majestic SEO, you can use our scraper suite tools for boiling them down further.

- *URL Filter Tool.* I use this to isolate the links and resource pages as these are often the best opportunities for what I promote. Input your backlinks into the input field and then add this string: resources?|links?|faqs|(web([^/]*)?) sites?|references? to the "Match Any" box. This will extract URLs that are most likely to be links pages.
- *One URL per Domain.* Once you have your probable links and resource pages, you should double-check that you have one per domain. Rarely is it "good form" to send two separate emails to a webmaster requesting links on two separate pages with broken links.
- *Backlink Checker.* Especially when using Majestic SEO's data, double-check that the pages still exist and that the links you're suggesting be changed are still actually on the pages. You can do this with the backlink checker that's a part of the scraper suite. Just copy in the domain of the dead page and paste in your list of suspects. The tool will show you on which pages the link still lives on.

WOW. That's right. Your list of prospects is now significantly diminished. You should be pretty happy when you still have between 50 and 80 real linking prospects to a now-dead resource. We have found upwards into the 1200s in the past. But even so, we're not ready to outreach; we still have to...

Pull Contact Info

Yes, the scraper suite does have a contact finder, but it won't solve all your problems. In fact, you may find it only around 25 to 30 percent accurate for contact info on links and resource pages (much better than nothing, for sure). It's great for blog contact finding, but the old, custom-CMS kinds of sites where links pages are commonly published don't always have standard ways of displaying contact info. There can even be tens or even hundreds of email addresses discovered with the tool for a given domain. This is why we have contractors whose sole job is to process the contact finder reports. They have to select the best email address or contact page and, when the tool doesn't find anything, go onsite to look for contact information. Last, they deliver a spreadsheet with two columns: URL where the dead link appears and contact information.

OUTREACH

Much has been written about broken-link building. Let's keep things short and sweet. Tell your contact where the broken link is and provide code for fixing it. Mention only one dead link on the page. If you're affiliated, say as much, though often assert that the person had some hand in writing the content.

As for conversions, be pleased with a 5-percent conversion rate but expect/plan/ prospect for a 2-percent conversion. I got 15-percent conversion once on a small-run, exact one-to-one replacement campaign in which the dead site had gotten parked. My outreach email told webmasters they were linking to a spam site. This is quite rare, but do note that the closer you can get to a one-to-one replacement, the better your results will be. Content recreation as a service is an interesting proposition but goes beyond the scope of this book on link building.

LINK EQUITY SALVAGE CAMPAIGNS

Link equity salvage is the process of finding and redirecting your site's dead pages, folders, and subdomains that still have links—sort of the reverse of the previous section on broken-link building. These are the old and mis-redirected, unredirected, or simply deleted sections of your site that webmaster tools doesn't know about since the URLs got axed more than 35 days ago.

We're talking about pages that even site crawlers aren't finding, presumably because they don't have any links from the visible pages of your site. And remember, link salvagers, you're not only recovering lost link equity here, but blocking competitive off-site link salvage experts from capitalizing on your squandered links.

You don't necessarily need to rush off hunting for onsite link salvage opportunities though—especially if your site's only a couple of years old and never had a redesign. If you can say yes to one or more of these criteria then definitely keep reading:

- Your site is more than five years old
- Your content naturally earns editorial links
- You've had one or more migrations from one content management system to another
- You've had several major site redesigns over the years
- You know of at least one mismanaged site redesign
- You have a 10,000-page site
- You aren't seeking targeted keyword ranking increases

I've broken the link equity salvage process into four parts: compiling, status checking, link checking a comprehensive-as-possible list of your site's URLs, and then redirecting them. The majority of the tools here are for compiling that critical master list of URLs.

Majestic SEO's Historic Index

Some folks complain of Majestic SEO's large quantity of dead links and pages. Don't be one of them.

- Look for quick wins thus. Place your root domain (no www) into Majestic SEO's Site Explorer.
- Click the Historic Index Radial. Then click Explore.
- Download your Top Links (shows highest-value links and the pages on your site they point to) and Top Pages CSVs.
- From both of these reports extract your site's URLs.

Dedupe. Boom. Presto. Pow! You now have a big list of the most important pages on your site, according to Majestic SEO.

You could also run a full-site report with Majestic SEO and get all your site's URLs that Majestic shows has an AC rank of 1 or higher. This costs more resources but provides a more thorough list.

Xenu's Link Sleuth

Xenu is a relentless beast of URL discovery, and it even status checks the URLs for you. It won't find every last URL, at least it hasn't in our tests, and it obviously can't find your legacy pages that still have links from offsite like Majestic SEO does. It finds only what's

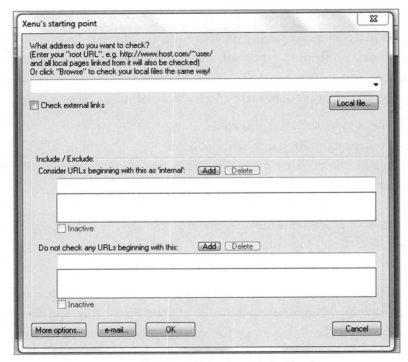

FIGURE 20–4. Xenu's Broken Link Checker

linked to onsite (as far as I understand how it works). Read "Checking Links with Xenu" for more information.

Xenu's Orphan Checker

We haven't used this on a client's site yet, only salivated at the opportunity to try it out and run a comparison to what can be found via Majestic SEO. Give Xenu's Orphan Checker FTP (File Transfer Protocol) access and it looks for pages on your server that are not linked to by any other pages on your own site.

Our guess is that the Orphan Checker isn't going to show you anything that's been flat-out deleted from your server, as can sometimes happen, so it's not a replacement for Majestic SEO. If you're on an obsessive hunt for link equity, it's worth a check.

Check Links Pages, Old Directories, and Press Releases

If your site has been getting editorial links and publishing press releases for years, you could have links to now-dead pages from pages that Majestic SEO may not have discovered. First you need to prospect for links pages and old press releases, and then check those pages for your domain with a bulk link checker.

Use Google Queries to Find Legacy Subdomains

Not every salvage requires a dead page—it could be a long-forgotten initiative prompted by an executive long gone from your organization. These subdomain-discovery queries, taught to me by Entrepreneur.com's SEO Jack Ngyuen, can help you find possibly abandoned subdomains.

- ■ *.domain.com
- ■ *.domain.com -inurl:www.
- ■ site:*.domain.com
- ■ site:*.domain.com -inurl:www.

Some of these queries work for some sites but not others. It depends on the size and/ or configuration of the site.

URL Status Checkers

Once you've compiled your insanely large list of URLs, it's time to check, recheck, and recheck their status codes. Yup, we advise at least three checks of a URL list, no matter what tool you're using.

One-off URL status checkers abound. You're going to need something with a bit more capacity. We know and love the bulk URL status checker built into our scraper suite.

Whatever tool you choose, it needs to work in bulk—large bulk. If it's on your desktop it could be tying up a machine for a few days. And remember—check your lists of failed URLs a couple more times. You'll always shake out more false positives.

Bulk Link Count Checkers

With your dead URLs in hand, it's time to separate the wheat from the chaff. This requires a bulk link checker—ideally one into which you can paste (potentially) thousands of dead URLs. We know of two. There are probably more, but these are the best known at the moment:

Majestic has a nifty "Bulk Backlink Checker" built in (with limits based on subscription level). If you've got 6,000 dead URLs to check, you could run it 20 times. Also, you can use our bulk backlink checker that accepts as many URLs as you can copy and paste in—it utilizes the Linkscape data set.

Once you get your data back from either tool, you can sort by number of referring domains and at last start the process of mapping and 301-redirecting your equity where it belongs.

Chapter 21

Bulk Outreach and Link Building

Because we hand-build links at relatively large scale, and always look for ways to go bigger, we continually test our link-building processes and beliefs. For example, when you have more than 80 guest posts to place in a month, you don't have the luxury to woo each and every prospect with commenting and tweeting (a common preciprocation warm-up tactic). To be sure, set aside a small handful of targets for relationship-based link building and then read this chapter on the principles of bulk outreach.

FROM LINK BUILDER TO EMAIL MARKETER

Link builder, it's time to think a bit differently. You are now an email marketer. Your task is not to build links, but rather to build lists, lists of relevant prospects and their contact information.

Then you must create an offer that will get these prospects to respond to you. Next you must lead them, often through further inbox dialogue, to take an action that will ultimately lead to a link, social distribution, and/ or more content that can attract more links.

LISTS OF PROSPECTS ARE EVERYWHERE

Though we still scrape SERPs for link prospects, we learned to supplement this method by searching for and scraping lists of websites. Sometimes I even look for lists first, and then brainstorm potential offers to make. Other times, I follow a hunch such as, "If I could find a list of hospitals, what could we offer them that could result in links?"

CREATE OFFERS THAT WORK AT SCALE

In bulk outreach, the ideal offer is one that's relatively unlimited. Guest posts—if you're pitching great content—are a bit limited. They can work but aren't ideal.

Free trials of web-based software? That's a bit less constrained. Widget installs? Ditto. Go to town!

Ask experts to take a survey? Unlimited—you make one survey and then conduct outreach. Remember—you must make certain that your offer genuinely appeals to the prospect list you've built, and that you'll get links in the process. Here are some examples of offers that scale:

- Free content (guest posting, infographics, widgets)
- Free products/services (for reviews and contests)
- Participation in expert survey (they answer questions, you publish answers, they link/share)
- Timely analysis and/or access to expertise (pitching a hot, topical interview with your expert)
- Philanthropy and fundraising participation (ask to spread the word, ask to pitch in too)
- Help fix broken, rotted, and now-parked links
- Money (not our bag, though some of our best friends are link buyers)

WRITE POWERFUL PITCH TEMPLATES

An effective offer, tailored to your target prospects, is 99 percent of a great pitch. That said, there are some key ingredients that your pitch should contain:

- Make your offer's benefits crystal clear.
- Make sure the pitch highlights benefits to publisher and their audience.
- Flaunt your brand. (I like to lead with brand in my first sentence if it's recognizable and OK with client . . .)
- Flaunt relevant success metrics. (My previous guest post got 700+ RTs! our last fundraiser netted over $5,000! Our last group interview got linked from Time. com!)

- Promote the page that contains your link. (I like offering to pay for traffic from StumbleUpon for guest posts.) A light dusting of your personality (this evolves for me over time, but can give the more relational-type prospects something to respond to).

SIMPLIFY YOUR PROSPECT QUALIFIERS

If your lists are targeted and relevant to your offers, then you have far less qualification work to do. In fact, your biggest problem should be taking the cream off the top for high-touch engagement rather than cutting out "the junk."

Part of the whole bulk outreach play is coming up with an offer that works across a spectrum of sites. For this reason, we propose that a principle qualifier for bulk outreach is whether you can scrape the contact information. With a contact finder tool you can see anywhere from 25 to 80 percent availability of contact info for sites depending on the vertical and how contactable the site owners want to be.

SIMPLIFY YOUR CAMPAIGN SUCCESS METRICS

Besides links earned (which isn't always that simple, anyway), email response rates (# of responses/# of emails) makes a strong indicator for bulk outreach campaigns. This tells you if you've pitched the benefits clearly and if your template is personable enough, and can give you a sense if you're even using the right offer.

We also recommend splitting your list and/or only sending to 5 to 10 percent of your list at first to allow for tuneups. Make sure you have someone who's "good in the inbox" for closing the emails that do come back—they need to be personable, chatty, and laser-focused on making those links happen. All of this comes out in the responses you get. Getting more responses helps you get more links.

EDUCATE YOURSELF ON CAN-SPAM

Here are some of the basic tenets of Can-Spam.

1. Don't use false or misleading header information.
2. Don't use deceptive subject lines.
3. Tell recipients where you're located.
4. Tell recipients how to opt out of receiving future email from you.
5. Honor opt-out requests promptly.
6. Monitor what others are doing on your behalf.

Since so much of link building is email marketing you'll definitely want to learn more than just the basics and how they apply to your exact situation.

Here's the best resource: www.business.ftc.gov/documents/bus61-can-spam-act-compliance-guide-business. It's easily found by searching for can-spam compliance in Google.

Chapter 22

How Reciprocal Links Can Be Viable

A reciprocal link is when two sites agree to give links to each other: I'll link to your site if you link to my site. But it's not quite that simple. People have tried to game the search engines with reciprocal links schemes, so the search engines have to look deeper to determine the intent of the reciprocity.

The rules of reciprocity cannot be perfectly defined. In other words, if you state that going beyond 30 percent reciprocity with your links is bad, I will tell you that's insane, besides being incorrect. Having a high reciprocity percentage (RP) is thought to be a red flag that the engines can use to devalue your links. The math is simple. If 100 percent of any site's inbound links are reciprocal, then those links can't really be trusted as an indicator of quality, because it could simply be a case of "you link to me and I'll link to you" (this can and does happen, but it isn't a quality-specific occurrence. Great sites do it, as do terrible ones. A great site that reciprocates links with other great sites does not harm itself in any way).

For some subjects, it is perfectly normal, almost expected, that the link reciprocity percentage should be extremely high, approaching 100. The more niche your subject matter, the more likely it is you will have a high RP with sites that have the same or similar subject matter.

Case in point? The Southeastern Bat Diversity Network, an organization with a goal to "conserve bats and their habitats in southeastern North

America through collaborative research, education, and management." (sbdn.org) Very noble indeed. I've always felt bats needed help.

If you take a look at other top sites within this subject area, you start to notice something. The other sites devoted to bats have a tendency to link back and forth to all the other sites devoted to bats. While this should not be surprising, many people miss a key point about what this means. Reciprocity link spam cannot be determined by a fixed number. A reciprocal links percentage cannot be set in stone. What's reciprocally spammy for one topic is perfectly natural in another.

Study the backlinks to a few related sites, such as BasciallyBats.org, Batcon.org, BatResearchNews, and North American Symposium on Bat Research (NASBR), and you see that each of these sites tends to link to the other, and vice versa. The reciprocal linking percentage across the top five sites is more than 80 percent, and for the top three, it's 100 percent. And this RP is perfectly natural, believable, and in no way an attempt to fool any algorithm or improve rank. These sites link to each other because they share the same passion for a very specific topic and want to make sure those people visiting and reading their content find the other sites about the same topic.

Now, if I examined five or ten sites devoted to another (broader) subject and found the same 80 percent or higher reciprocity rate, that would be suspicious. For example, if the subject matter is NFL jerseys, where hundreds of sites fight for SEO supremacy, it would be an absolute red flag for the engines if we found any ten NFL jersey sites linking back and forth to each other with the same high RP as our bat example.

In fact, I'd argue that 80 percent reciprocity among a collection of NFL jersey sites was a signal they might just be operated by the same people. That's the very definition of a link network and link spam, yet the RP was no different than my bat examples. The only difference was the subject matter.

Let's rephrase and repeat that.

The RP was no different between my bat example and my NFL jersey example. The only difference was the subject matter.

Which brings us to those absolutes. You simply cannot make any sort of absolute statement as to what constitutes reciprocal link spam. Nor can you say that reciprocal links are always good, always bad, always suspicious, always helpful. They are never any of these, and they are always all of these. What you have to do is look at each case, at each site, and recognize the logical, natural linking potential and reciprocity tendencies.

It's not rocket science, either. Some of what you just read seems so obvious to longtime link builders that it's easy to forget. The cult of reciprocal links advocates and enemies would do well to call a truce and stop looking for absolutes, and start looking for illustrative examples to help each site know if, how, and when to implement reciprocal links properly, or at all.

Chapter 23

Link-Building Tools

Link Insight is one of several search and advertising intelligence tools created by Rich Stokes's team at AdGooroo.com. Rich is a visionary and fellow author, having penned *The Ultimate Guide to Pay-Per-Click Advertising* for Entrepreneur Press. You will benefit from both Rich's book and Link Insight.

MORE ABOUT LINK INSIGHT

The mission of Link Insight is to find inbound links both to your site as well as up to nine of your competitors. At any given time, this process results in a set of tens or hundreds of thousands of potential backlinks—far too large a list for the average team outreach. Link Insight takes it a step further: It analyzes every page and gives each backlink four grades: TrustSignal, SocialSignal, GeoSignal, or SpamSignal. These four simple signals tell you how effective or risky each potential link is before you spend precious time pursuing them. Link Insight designers have evaluated hundreds of thousands of links over the years and helped establish some of the biggest brands on the web. The result? A small set of high-potential links that can help build both your website's traffic as well as its trust and authority. And in the process, you'll avoid wasting time and money with such bad ideas as link exchanges, sponsored links, forum and comment spam, and other techniques used by companies engaging in black-hat SEO.

To learn more about Link Insight, visit http://www.adgooroo.com/products/link_insight.php.

MAJESTIC SEO SITE EXPLORER

Majestic SEO is one of the handfuls of tools that have attempted to record all the links on the internet. There have been others crazy enough to attempt this to be sure—Ahrefs.com, SEOMoz, and of course, Google itself. But Majestic SEO has gradually become our go-to backlink graph, beating the others out for its fresh-enough results and extensive history (it goes back to 2006).

So here's how we use it.

Competitive Backlink Analysis

Majestic SEO provides a quick glimpse at competitors' unique inbound linking domains. Just paste in their root domain (the URL with no http:// or www. at the beginning). This provides you with a quick and dirty idea of the amount of work you'll have to do in order to compete. Be sure to look at their top pages, too, by clicking the "Top Pages" tab. This shows which pages have the most valuable links.

Furthermore, it's possible to cherry-pick links that your competitors have earned and approach the sites on your own. Note that using competitor link analysis for prospecting is not particularly scalable. It could be a great one-to-five-hour project for an inhouse SEO, though!

Bulk Backlink Checker

When you've found a batch of dead pages or sites, submit them all to the bulk link checker and set it to return results based on linking domains. Presto! You've got a list of dead sites or pages ordered by the number of inbound linking domains.

Find Links to Dead Pages

We haven't taken the time to master their reports, so I'm stuck with the top 5,000 backlinks. And this will include all the backlinks from a single domain. Typically in batches of 5,000 there are between 1,000 and 2,500 unique domains. Of those, usually between 500 and 1,000 are still actually live with links on them.

Find Links Pages for Dead Site Discovery

Start with a .gov site in your conceptual neighborhood (fda.gov for a health site) and then download links just to its home page. Then look in the URL strings for the words "links" or "resources." This will help you find hundreds of topical links pages that will undoubtedly contain some dead sites or pages.

New Link Reporting

In broken-link building in particular it isn't always easy to find the results of your handiwork—primarily because the page you request a link on isn't where you always end up. Since Majestic SEO is updated so frequently, you'll often find new links on pages you didn't target, but from domains you did. If you are working on a projects that requires you acquire times links per month, this is vital. Note: ahrefs.com (paid version) can be used for this purpose as well—their index gets updated daily.

KEYWORD COMBINER

We still use the heck out of a keyword combiner tool, for combining prospecting phrases rather than SEO keywords. There's one built into the link prospector but the one in our Chrome toolbar is Keyword Combination Tool http://www.npresence.net/Keyword-Combination-Tool.html.

Be warned though, some keyword combiners don't allow for quotation marks or other advanced operators. And the one linked to here is defaulted to doing a double combo.

UBERSUGGEST

This wonderful tool scrapes Google's suggestions, giving link prospectors instant access to the "problem space" around a given phrase. This is useful particularly at the early stages of a campaign. Sign up at http://ubersuggest.org.

Test it out with something like: "how do I" to get an idea of what it does. Then narrow in on your space. For example, try "link building for," which leads Ubersuggest into helping you discover what people are actively searching for.

FIGURE 23–1. Ubersuggest

THE URL STATUS CHECKER

This one's dead-dumb simple. Input a list of URLs you want to check and then hit submit. You will need to check your dead URLs a couple of times and still end up weeding through a few false positives.

REGEX FILTERING TOOL

Back in the Majestic SEO section on page 156 we describe pulling backlinks to authority sites and sifting through them for links and resource pages. This nifty little filter tool provides regular expressions for this.

PICK SHORTEST URL PER DOMAIN

Sometimes you only need one URL from a domain, but you have hundreds (all mixed in with URLs from other domains). This free tool (login required) picks the shortest URL per domain and dumps the rest. Good for cleaning up lists of possible outreach targets.

LIST COMPARISON TOOL—http://jura.wi.mit.edu/bioc/tools/compare.php

Sometimes you need to de-dupe two lists without combining them. For this you need to use the list comparison tool. This thing can handle tens of thousands of URLs at a time. We've never pushed it farther than that—hopefully it doesn't get shut down after sharing it here!

THE SUPER DEDUPER—www.dedupelist.com

Actually it's called just the "DeDupeList tool," but we prefer "Super DeDuper. This tool removes duplicates from lists of URLs, but be sure to remove the www. from your list first or you'll still have multiple instances of the same domain.

THE CONTACT FINDER—http://tools.citationlabs.com

This tool (paid) finds between 20 and 80 percent of contacts from a list of URLs. Hand off the output of this tool to your human contact-finding team to handle the email address selection and to go site by site to find the rest.

ARCHIVE.ORG

While anchor text can provide ample clues about the content of a page or site, nothing beats Archive.org for piecing together the purpose of a page. Some BLB outfits repurpose content from Archive.org.

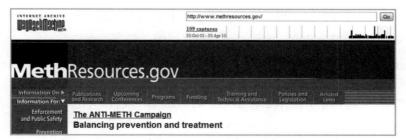

FIGURE 23–2. The Internet Archive, aka Wayback Machine

THE URL OPENER—www.urlopener.com/index.php

Numerous tools can open multiple tabs in your browser when hand-qualifying sites. Try to hand-qualify as little as possible these days, but when you need to, use the URL opener (also made by the Super DeDuper guy).

THE LINK PROSPECTOR TOOL

The link prospector (a tool we built for our link prospecting work at Citation Labs) is the only commercially available tool for large-scale and highly flexible prospecting in any language. The following walkthrough provides tips on mastering the tool.

Choose Your Link-Building Tactic

After creating a new campaign for your account (campaigns are essentially "folders" for organizing your link prospects) it's time to click "Find Prospects" and pick a report type (see Figure 23–3). The report types in the Link Prospector are roughly organized around

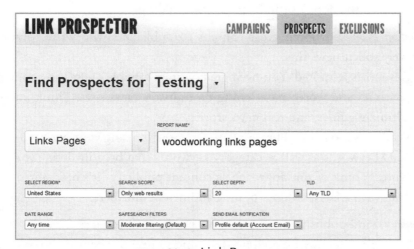

FIGURE 23–3. Link Prospector

tactics. Here is a list of the report types, the tactics they support, the resources you're likely to need, and any notes.

1. *Guest Posting.* You write and pitch content to publishers. This content includes links to your website.
   - Resources Required: you will need writers, sources for great (or at least publishable) ideas and *lots* of prospects.
   - Productive Research Phrases: Experiment with using your big-head to mid-tail SEO keywords as well as category keywords that broadly define your market. For example, use "heart health" instead of "Philips HeartStart Home Defibrillator." Do try both though—you never know what might turn up!
   - Notes: This method typically requires large numbers of guest posts to be effective. Set aside the majority of your prospects for content you spend less time on—especially if these sites don't seem to have large readerships. For larger, better-known sites expect to spend more time on content and look for more referral traffic and brand impact.

2. *Links Pages.* The tactic here is typically "begging" for or "requesting" links to your content.
   - Resources Required: Fantastic, noncommercial informative content and a stellar outreach person who also happens to be great at sales.
   - Productive Research Phrases: Experiment with using your big-head to mid-tail SEO keywords as well as category keywords that broadly define your market.
   - Notes: Legitimate links pages rarely occur at scale and you'll find better success if you look for the pages first, see what actually earns links, and make sure what you're pitching really fits there. Broken link building is another great "foot in the door" for links-page link building.

3. *Content Promoters.* Pitch great content to publishers who write roundups and actively solicit news tips.
   - Resources Required: You need great writers capable of creating content that's "with it" and worth mentioning on industry news sites. Think infographics, ultimate guides, and real news stories.
   - Productive Research Phrases: Experiment with using your big-head to mid-tail SEO keywords as well as category keywords that broadly define your market.
   - Notes: Think of this approach as content publicity—it's best suited for industries with a large number of blog and news publishers.

4. *Reviews.* Find publishers to review your products or services.
   - Resources Required: You'll need products or service bandwidth to give away.

- Productive Research Phrases: Try product categories as well as competitors' brand names (that have been extensively reviewed).
- Notes: For the link prospector, reviews have been the single best source of new sales—not to mention links.

5. *Giveaways*. Find publishers to give away your products or services in a contest.
   - Resources Required: You'll need products or service bandwidth to give away.
   - Productive Research Phrases: Try product/service categories as well as competitors' brand names (that you know have used the contest tactic).
   - Notes: Typically giveaways and contests require some compensation for the publisher.

6. *Donations*. Sponsor charities and other organizations that run on donations.
   - Resources Required: Money, goods, or services. But usually money.
   - Productive Research Phrases: Here you want to stay far away from your SEO or even category terms. Instead try condition terms such as "homelessness," or what-it-is terms like "animal shelter." Alternatively you can use geo-terms like the state or city or even neighborhood you'd like to concentrate on.
   - Notes: You may have to negotiate and educate a bit for the link—not all sites are used to the idea of providing them.

7. *Commenting*. Join the conversation on blog posts and articles that discuss relevant topics.
   - Resources Required: Someone with enough knowledge to add value to a discussion and not just drop links.
   - Productive Research Phrases: Experiment with using your big-head to mid-tail SEO keywords as well as category keywords that broadly define your market.
   - Notes: This tactic is as much for the links as it is for a nice shot of relevant traffic to resources on your site.

8. *Expert Interviews*. Find experts to interview on your site—or the writers that interview them.
   - Resources Required: You will need someone with enough expertise to get writers interested in interviewing them. Or you'll need some great questions to ask other experts in your industry (with the hope of getting links from them as well as their followers).
   - Productive Research Phrases: Use category keywords that broadly define your market at first, and then move on to commonly interviewed experts.
   - Notes: Assemble several experts and conduct a group expert interview.

9. *Directories.* Find sites that attempt to catalog all of the websites on the internet—or their niche.
   - Resources Required: You need someone to submit to the directories and a bit of money as well. Some niche directories can get quite expensive.
   - Productive Research Phrases: Use category keywords that broadly define your market as well as any niche keywords that may relate.
   - Notes: Directories are considered by most to be foundational link building.

10. *Forums.* Invest time and educate a pre-existing community of passionate users.
    - Resources Required: Someone who can educate without selling.
    - Productive Research Phrases: Use category keywords that broadly define your market.
    - Notes: This tactic is ideally more of a long-term investment in a community than a quick-links tactic. It will take time to earn trust. So make sure that the community or communities you're targeting are large enough to get you a return on your time.

11. *Topical Blogs.* Outreach and engage with bloggers from your industry.
    - Resources Required: This will depend on how you plan to engage, whether via content promotion, guest posting, contests, or news story pitches.
    - Productive Research Phrases: Use category keywords that broadly define your market.
    - Notes: This is the best way to find sites for guest posting that don't necessarily call them guest posts.

12. *Professional Organizations.* Joining industry trade organizations can help build links and credibility.
    - Resources Required: Money, sometimes service hours.
    - Productive Research Phrases: Use trade phrases that define the practitioners in your industry.
    - Notes: Like directories, professional organizations fall into a "foundational" category. You will likely burn through those available fairly quickly, but they're worth checking for.

13. *Research Content.* Search for your market's how-to content so you can find out what informational needs you can meet.
    - Resources Required: Research time and a content writer.
    - Productive Research Phrases: Use category keywords that broadly define your market.

- Notes: When you create content based on existing resources, be sure to send an email to the site you're linking to and let them know.

14. *Custom.* For any tactics not mentioned above, select "custom."
    - Resources Required: This will vary based on your creativity and understanding of prospecting.
    - Productive Research Phrases: Review Chapter 8 about link prospecting with queries.
    - Notes: The Custom Report Type enables prospecting in non-English languages. You will have to create your own prospecting phrases in your language first though!

Finding Highly Productive Research Phrases

The Link Prospector takes your research phrases and combines them with tactic-specific footprints. This is what we use to find prospects for you. Your research phrases determine how useful and relevant your prospects will be. What's tricky about research phrases is what works for one tactic may not work for another. Productive research phrases for donation opportunities may not be productive for guest-posting opportunities. That said, there are only three set rules for selecting your research phrases: Try, but don't rely, solely on your SEO keywords; test research phrases in Google before adding to the prospector; and experiment!

Try But Don't Rely on SEO Keywords

Many SEOs start prospecting with their target keywords. Those are the terms they want to rank for, so why not use them for prospecting? We used to tell people to never use their SEO keywords, but soon realized that there are cases where they *can* yield good results. So now we simply say—test them, but don't rely on them solely for every report type.

If you read through the tactical report overview, you'll notice that the most recommended research phrases are category keywords that define a vertical. If you're selling defibrillators, use "heart health" as a starting point for research, for example. Alternatively, the big-head phrases in your vertical can prove productive.

Test Research Phrases in Google

It's easy to test research phrases in Google—and it's a great way to find other potentially productive research phrases, too. To test a research phrase, simply type it into Google and then add the tactic or report type you're prospecting for. So, if you're pursuing guest posting, type Test [keyword] guest post into Google. If you see four to five "maybes" in the top ten results, then you've got a winner. If you see none, then dump it.

And do watch those SERPs closely as you test—that's where you'll notice new potential research phrases. The beauty here is in how simple it is to test. And what you'll find when you test your research phrases first (before adding them to a query) is that you spend less time qualifying your prospects. More of them will be useful.

When you *do* find a productive word, you can try this query to shake up new phrases: ~[keyword]-[keyword]. This is essentially asking Google to return phrases to you that are synonyms to your productive phrase, but *not* your productive phrase. The tilde and the minus sign are both advanced operators.

Last, if you find productive two-to-three word phrases, you might want to add them to the Link Prospector both with and without quotes as this will help to float up new potential domains.

Experiment!

There's no substitution for testing, experimenting, and just plain "seeing what happens." Every time we make a rule we find that it can be overturned in certain cases or for certain report types. Though it takes longer, and will cost you a bit more in terms of credits, we suggest you try out as many variations as possible, and never stop questioning what you know. This does admittedly make training tricky. That said, when we ask contractors to prospect before training and *then* ask them to explain what they're looking for and the research phrase decisions they made along the way, we are surprised by what we learn.

Research phrases are a tricky and slippery subject. Keep testing and experimenting and you'll find your results get more and more productive!

Setting the Advanced Targeting Parameters for Useful Prospects

Once you've selected your report type and found some productive research phrases, it's time to "dial in" your prospects with the Link Prospector's Advanced Targeting Parameters. Setting the parameters can help reduce your time spent qualifying your results by "weeding out" or narrowing the nonprospects before you even download your results.

Note: You can (and at first, probably should) leave your parameters set to their defaults, and you'll still find great results. That said, familiarity with the parameters will help you enormously as you learn more about what is and isn't a prospect for your given tactic.

Report Types

We covered report types earlier, but we'll touch on them again as they're vital for using the tool productively. The report types are primarily organized by "tactic," that is, the manner by which you intend to engage with publishers to earn mentions or links. The Custom Report enables you to pass queries in bulk directly to the search engine.

Select Region

By selecting the region, you specify which top-level domain (TLD) of search engine from which you'd like to source your prospects. If you'd like prospects geared toward a UK market, select "United Kingdom." If you'd like German-oriented prospects, select "Germany." Please note: If you're looking for non-English prospects you should *not* use the preset reports. You must use the Custom Report type and design your own prospecting queries. Please contact us; we're happy to assist in this process.

Search Scope

Search Scope enables you to pull prospects from either web results or blog results. We rarely recommend using both, unless you're specifically looking for blogs and want to be as thorough as possible.

Select Depth

Depth refers to the number of results that you will attempt to return from the search engines. Depth does *not* refer to the number of pages of results! You can look for 1 through 1,000 results for you, but we recommend for most prospecting jobs that you set your depth to 10 or 20. This is because there are rarely productive prospects past the 20 result.

TLD

TLD enables you to limit your prospects based on the TLD of the domains, e.g., .edu, .gov, .org. You can also input TLDs that are not included in the drop-down menu. Alternatively you can just add site:.[tldofchoice] to your research phrase fields.

Date Range

"Date Range" enables you to limit your prospects based on the time frame within which they were indexed. This is especially useful for guest posting—set the Date Range to "past year" so you can find the sites that have published a guest post within the last year. Commenting ops benefit from freshness—select "past 30 days" to find pages that are more recent and therefore more likely to have an open conversation.

Safesearch Features

"Safesearch" enables you to pre-remove results that are potentially shocking or offensive. Some people prefer not to scan through results to ensure they are "safe for work" enough to pass along to clients, and Safesearch helps with this.

Send Email Notification

Once your report is complete, you can designate who receives a notification via email. You can also set it so that no one receives an email. If you'd like to permanently set this, you can do so in the "Profile" section.

Exclude Domains

"Exclude Domains" enables you to remove a list of domains at the global and/or campaign level—you have to set them up before they can be excluded, though! Click the "Exclusions" tab to manage them and note the syntax of exclusions: *.domain.com excludes the domain along with any subdomain that could occur.

Research Phrases

Your research phrases are the most powerful way to direct the tool's results. Here's more about selecting productive research phrases.

We recommend using category, or big-head, phrases here rather than your targeted SEO keywords. For example, rather than "Harley Davidson XR1200X" we recommend using "motorcycle." Above all, though, we recommend experimenting and assumption testing!

Exporting and Qualifying Your Link Prospects

Congratulations, link prospector—you're moving right along! By now you've selected your tactic, identified some productive prospecting phrases, and dialed in your parameters. Our hope is that you remembered to hit the big blue "Submit" button at the bottom of the Find Prospects page. If so, you will have prospects in about 10 to 20 minutes (though it could be more if you've adjusted your parameters significantly).

When your prospects are ready you'll receive an email notification. You can click through directly from the email to view your report. Alternatively, log in to your account, hover your cursor over the Prospects tab, and click "View Prospects." You may have to designate the campaign for which you'd like to view prospects.

Export Domains vs. Export Paths

On the Prospects page you have two download options—"Domains" or "Paths." Paths are the long URLs we found, the entire URL of the opportunity. Domains are just that— the domain where we found the page that looks like an opportunity. Deciding which one to download depends on what tactic you're pursuing.

If you're hunting for guest-posting opportunities, you don't necessarily need to see the actual page where a guest post exists, but rather the homepage of the site itself. Therefore you should download the domains.

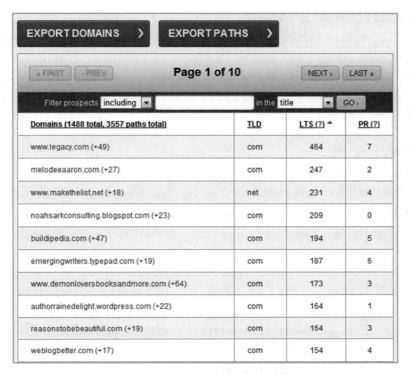

FIGURE 23–4. Domain Exporting

If you're looking for links pages, then simply knowing the domain where the links page exists is not enough—you need to know the location of the links page itself. In this case, you should download the paths.

Qualify by Existing Metrics

We provide PageRank data for domains as well as our own home-brewed "LTS" (Link Target Score) score. They are very different numbers and enable you to make educated guesses about very different types of prospects. The LTS score is calculated on a per-report basis. The score is a measurement of the relevance of a given domain to the prospecting queries that the tool ran on your behalf. If your research phrases were productive, then this score can help you set a lower threshold of "by-eye checking." That said, the threshold will be different for every report, so there's really no absolute number we can advise for you to make decisions on. PageRank, too, can help make sweeping decisions, and its benefit over LTS is that it *is* relatively absolute, so you can compare prospects from one report to another. All that said, we rarely make final outreach decisions (yes, we will outreach to this prospect or no, we will not) based on either one of these metrics (or any one metric).

Search the Paths Download Spreadsheet

The "Paths" download includes titles and meta snippets for each of the prospective URLs. So in addition to qualifying by PageRank or LTS, you can simply search your path's CSV file for the appearance of words you believe will imply a quality prospect. This is especially effective for isolating links pages that have the word "link" in either the title or meta descriptions (but not the URL).

Regular Expressions

They're not that scary when you use a tool, we promise! Over in the Citation Labs' "Scraper Suite" we have a handful of free, registration-required tools including our "URL Filter" After you register and log in, navigate to the Tools menu, click Free Utilities, and then URL Filter. Paste in a large batch of URLs—the more the merrier— and remember the following syntax: [keyword] or [keyword1|keyword2|keyword3]. Now you add your keywords to the Any, All, or None fields on the right side of the screen. "Match Any" means the tool will show results that have any of these keywords (keyword1|keyword2|keyword3) in the URL. "Match All" means the URLs must contain all of these keywords (keyword1|keyword2|keyword3). "Match None" means that these keywords (keyword1|keyword2|keyword3, etc.) must *not* appear in the URLs.

It's especially useful for making fast decisions about huge batches of URLs. Here's what to add to "Match Any" to sort links pages out of a huge list of URLs:

resources?|links?|faqs|(web([^/]*)?)sites?|references?

If you're in a huge hurry you can just use links|resources.

Using regular expressions with this tool means you'll only be looking at the URLs, so any pages that don't use title tags or real words in the URL will be filtered out.

Qualify URLs "By Eye" in the Spreadsheet

After you've been prospecting and link building for years, you'll get to trust your ability to go through a list of URLs quickly by eye. Some people can burn through a few hundred in ten minutes or so. It's taxing, but it's important primarily because there are so many prospects that are easy to miss if you rely on metrics or regular expressions. We suggest you create a column named "Maybe" in your report. Scan the list of URLs and place a one in that column if you look at the URL and can't see a quick and easy reason to say no. Then sort by that column. Note: It's by going through spreadsheets by hand that you'll become knowledgeable about what keywords to use for regular expressions. And you may just come up with some new, productive research phrases while you're at it.

Visit the Page

It's not necessary to do this for every prospect; that said, never send a batch of prospects over to the contact-gathering phase without visiting some of them, just to get a feel for what you're working with and to ensure that there's going to be offer/prospect alignment. Visiting some pages—spot checking, if you will—provides you with potential signs that you need to adjust course.

Track Your Nonlink-Opportunity Domains

As you work you'll come across domains that you never, ever need to see again. Garbage. And those domains will keep popping up forever unless you add them to your campaign or global exclusions. Do yourself a huge favor and remove them. To exclude just the domain, you have to add www.domain.com as well as domain.com. To exclude the domain and all its subdomains, add *.domain.com. *.blogspot.com, for example, would exclude all Blogspot blogs from your reports.

Chapter 24

Six Link-Building Lessons from Our Peers

Now for some field experience from six professionals using the link-building tools and methods discussed earlier.

BRUCE CLAY

Bruce Clay Inc. (BCI, www.bruceclay.com) is an internet marketing optimization company providing SEO services, PPC advertising management, SEO-friendly web design and information architecture, and social media and conversion-rate optimization services. BCI is also the creator of the award-winning SEOToolSet® and its acclaimed SEO training course.

Bruce Clay has led the search marketing industry since 1996 through contributions such as the SEO Code of Ethics, Search Engine Relationship Chart®, and SEO training and certification programs that promote ethical SEO practices. Headquartered in California, Bruce Clay Inc. has global locations in Australia, Switzerland, India, Japan, and Brazil.

Infographics, Links, and Linkbait by Bruce Clay

Back in the late 1990s, when we were all fighting to understand how to get websites indexed by the search engines, it became obvious that a map was

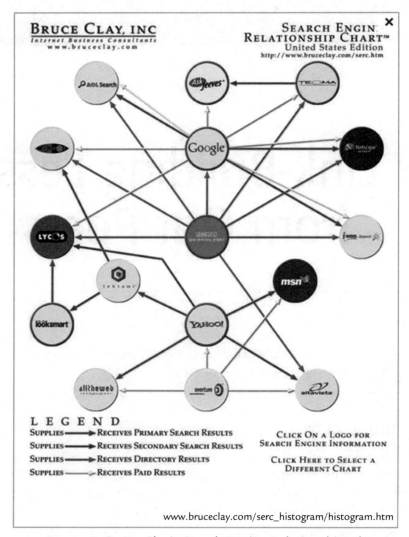

FIGURE 24–1. Bruce Clay's Search Engine Relationship Chart

needed. And as there were no maps that helped us with this we decided to develop our own data-mapping diagram.

The first Search Engine Relationship Chart (SERC) took weeks to research and assemble. Once we had the data it was a matter of deciding to publish our SERC. As the first industry infographic we published it as a PDF. We posted information in the major email newsletters of the time complete with the download link, and within no time the PDF was downloaded more than 300,000 times. We were happy to have our chart on the wall of colleagues nationwide, and especially our brand. This was singularly the most successful branding and visibility program we have ever done. Now, with more than a score of follow-on versions, we are finding the attraction of the chart waning, but for 11 years we did certainly have a great run. The SERC was a landmark of every SEO office, and we are proud to have been the firm that developed and provided it for all these years.

CHRISTINE CHURCHILL

Christine Churchill, the president of KeyRelevance (www.keyrelevance.com), is a recognized expert in the field of search engine marketing. She is a strong advocate for ethical search engine marketing and was a member of the founding board of directors of the Search Engine Marketing Professional Organization (SEMPO).

Christine serves on the board of directors of the Dallas-Fort Worth Search Engine Marketing Association. She holds a master's degree in business and has more than ten years of online marketing experience.

Christine is a regular speaker at Search Marketing Expo, Search Engine Strategies, Webmaster World Publishers Conference, High Rankings Seminars, Internet World, and other internet conferences. In addition, she has written widely on search engine marketing for publications including *SearchDay, MarketPosition, Workz, SitePoint, SearchEngineGuide*, and *NetMechanic,* and has taught SEO classes through the Direct Marketing Association and International Association of Webmasters. Christine is also a trainer for the SMX Bootcamp sessions and Search Engine Strategies for their four-hour Keyword Research and Paid Search Training classes.

Using Paid Search to Support Link-Building Efforts by Christine Churchill

Paid search can be used in a variety of ways to support link building. Here are some ideas to help you identify keywords and possible link partners using paid advertising.

Paid Search as Part of Keyword Research

Pay-per-click advertising has long been a favorite way for search marketers to acquire real performance data on keywords. While keyword tools can provide lists of relevant keywords, the best way to really know which keywords perform best for your site is to test their performance in a paid search campaign. This requires a fair amount of effort to ensure that this is a legitimate test, in that in addition to coming up with the keywords, you would also need to develop effective ad copy and landing pages to support the test.

Paid search combined with conversion tracking gives the search marketer information on exactly which terms work best for the site. If you know certain terms are popular and, more importantly, convert well, you would want to target them both in your paid and organic optimization as well as your link-building efforts.

With Google now encrypting search for logged-on users, the information provided by a site's analytics data on organic queries will be limited. Webmasters looking at their analytics will no longer receive referring data on keywords used to bring users who were signed in to Google when they clicked on a search results page. While Google claims that the number of users signed in is very small, many sites are reporting that their analytics are displaying "not provided" where their main keywords used to show. Since Google is encouraging users to log in, the trend to search while logged in will continue to increase, further limiting the availability of organic keyword data over time. Going forward, the best referring keyword data and keyword performance data will be from paid search.

Paid Search as a Way to Find Linking Partners

The best link partners are sites that are related to your site. Specifically the best link partner sites are sites that are complementary to your industry but not a direct competitor. One way to identify complementary sites is to do keyword searches on terms related to your main terms and look for sites that show up in the search results that aren't competitors. For example, if you sold shoe accessories, you might want to be aware of sites selling women's shoes.

If you search on a term related to your main term, scan over the sites showing up in the paid listings. Often you see the big brands showing up in the organic top results and the top paid results, but if you look down below the fold, you often find sites that are off your radar. These could be sites that are viable companies related to your business but are not competitors. A quick review of these sites would tell you if they sell related complementary products but are not competition in your space. If they are not competitors, these sites could be potential business and link partners.

Serious businesses are more likely to be found by analyzing the paid search advertisers, since they have the resources to be paying to bring clients to their sites. As such, these will make better potential linking partners.

Look for Ads on Content Sites as a Way to Discover Link Partners

Here's another tip to help you find potential link partners. In this case, you aren't actually spending money on paid search, but rather looking for content sites that use Google AdSense or another paid search advertising network. AdSense is Google's program for publishers where Google allows sites to put some code on pages of their site, which Google then uses to place relevant ads on the page. Publishers are paid by Google for the click-throughs the ads receive.

Many content publishers' sites rank well for terms related to your business keywords. If you review the search results pages for content sites related to your business, you might find sites that are financed by AdSense ads. Webmasters of these sites have monetized their site and may be more open to developing a business relationship with your site.

Business deals can take a variety of shapes. If you have an affiliate program, they may want to become an affiliate. They may allow you to sponsor a section of their site or they may even agree to place your ad on their site. Don't worry that the ad may be a no-follow link. It may be that this site turns out to be a great traffic site or a great converting site for you. If that is the case, the link is valuable to you whether it is a follow or not.

Other business relationship options might be offering a guest blogging post, an interview, or have them review one of your products. Again, don't get wrapped around the no-follow issue. Links are part of a business relationship. Some of the best links you'll ever get from a business perspective will be no-follow links from a related site.

DEBRA MASTALER

Based in Fairfax Station, Virginia, Debra Mastaler is president of Alliance-Link (www. alliance-link.com), an interactive marketing company focused on providing custom link-building training and consultations. In business since 2000, Debra and her talented staff offer a common-sense approach to link building by combining traditional sales and promotional strategies with effective online search engine marketing tactics. In addition to client projects and link training for Fortune 500 companies as well as a number of top SEO firms in the USA, U.K., and Canada, Debra is a featured guest speaker at the Search Engine Strategies Conference (SES) and Search Marketing Expo (SMX), a guest blogger for Search Engine Land and Search Engine Guide, and has done numerous High Ranking Seminars, Small Business Unleashed Seminars as well as the Link Building Training sessions for SES, SMX, and the Direct Marketing Association (DMA). Debra is also the link-building moderator on the SEO Book Community Forums (www.seobook. com) and has moderated similar categories on the Small Business Ideas Forum and Sphinn. In 2009 Debra was listed 17th in the Top 100 Most Influential Marketers (as voted by invesp.net).

Directory Links—Are They Worth It? by Debra Mastaler

Ask ten link builders if directory links are worth the time and effort to secure, and you'll get ten different answers. I think they are and can be a viable part of your linking mix provided you consider a number of key elements when using them.

If you've spent any time in/around the SEO industry, you know there are hundreds, if not thousands of small directories online; most of these sites lack editorial guidelines and were created to host AdSense and network links. I think it's important to draw a distinction between these sites and the responsible, well-run directories that I, and most link builders I know, use.

What Is a Directory?

In short, a directory is a collection of websites categorized by subject and/or geographic location. Human reviewers determine what source will be added and also maintain the directory and its structure. You're probably very familiar with the following four directories; all have been online for a very long time and have strong editorial guidelines:

- The World Wide Web Virtual Library or VLIB (1991)
- The Yahoo! Directory (1994)
- Best of the Web (1994)
- Open Directory Project/DMOZ (1998)

Each employs human reviewers to look at the sites submitted and determine which category they should be placed in. This process of being scrutinized to determine acceptance is known as editorial review and is why these and other directories are respected algorithmically by the search engines.

It is difficult to get a site listed with the DMOZ and VLIB; follow their submission guidelines and take care to add your site to the right category. Even if you're unsuccessful in getting in, you can use the sites and resources listed in these directories and mine them for link partners.

Is This a Good Directory?

If you come across a directory and want to add your site, ask yourself these questions before handing over your submission fee:

- Does the directory have minimal/no AdSense on category pages? Adsense ads detract from your listing; I shy away from a directory that hosts ads on my category page.
- Does the directory support sitewide links? Directories created to support manipulative linking go against the search engine TOS; I'd stay away from them.
- Does the directory have full contact information available and/or an "About Us" page? Look for a directory owned by a reputable company, one that will answer your questions and be available if you need help.
- Is your category page in the Google and Bing index and are the pages of your category cached frequently? If the page your link/site will be added to is not in the search index, you'll see no benefit.

Directory Submission Tactics as a Business Model

If you owned a business on Main Street and wanted to promote it to the community, it's doubtful you'd use just one advertising method to get your message across. You'd probably begin with the basic, less expensive options such as buying ads in the Yellow Pages, your local newspaper, and Valpak mailers. Eventually you'd move up and buy radio, TV, and sponsorship opportunities, which will help make you a dominant presence in your community.

This scattershot approach to building a credible reputation can be done online as well. I advocate using directory links in the first wave of linking as a way to jump-start your linking program. Granted, they're not algorithmic giants, but directory links will pass link popularity and add to your overall backlink profile.

RAND FISHKIN

Rand is the CEO of SEO software company SEOmoz (http://www.SEOmoz.org). He co-wrote *The Art of SEO* published by O'Reilly Media, co-founded Inbound.org, and was named on *PSBJ*'s "40 Under 40" list and *BusinessWeek* "30 Best Tech Entrepreneurs Under 30." Rand is an addict of all things content and social on the web, from his multiple blogs to Twitter, Google+, Facebook, LinkedIn, FourSquare, and even a bit of Pinterest. In his minuscule spare time, Rand enjoys the company of his amazing wife, whose serendipitous travel blog chronicles their journeys.

Five of My Top Link-Building Tips by Rand Fishkin

The following are specific tactics, all designed to generate high-quality inbound links (often accompanied by social media shares) that can potentially send traffic, increase search engine value, and are entirely editorial/white hat.

1. *Build a "Top X Blogs/Sites/People" in Your Industry*
   Curating a list of great sites and/or people always gets attention from audiences seeking to learn more about the field. It also frequently earns tremendous links because those listed share their position/notoriety both via temporal media like Twitter, Facebook, or Google+ as well as in their bios or About pages (which often make their way to third-party sites as well). The bigger and more respectable your brand grows, the more links and attention these lists can attract.

2. *Create Content That Adds Value to Prominent Conversations*
   The web world is filled with content taking sides on virtually every issue in almost any topical arena. Participating in these "conversations" by adding an intelligent

voice with valuable research, a well-thought-out opinion, and quality writing will often earn you a place in the debate, which yields links and social shares. Over time, if you stick to participating honestly and appropriately, you'll earn a following of your own and a place in the online media world around your topic. Just be careful not to get too caustic or emotional—the internet's discussions can get rough and not everyone plays nicely (which is another reason measured responses and clear heads can earn links from positive participation).

3. *Collect and Publish Unique Information in a Link-Friendly Format (and Prime the Pump Beforehand)*

Aggregated information is tough to come by, but often incredibly valuable and link-worthy. The problem is that someone needs to do the legwork to assemble the aggregated material—that's where you come in. Whether it's the opinions of major bloggers in a field, the statistics from visit data, the various perspectives on how an event occurred or polling data from a hard-to-find set of companies/professionals/individuals, your marketing acumen plus some sweat equity can bring in the numbers. Once you have, building a link-worthy collection of graphs, charts, presentations, video, or even bullet points in a well-executed article can have terrific returns in links and social shares. You can earn additional value by leveraging those who contribute their data/responses to help spread the word—and most will, given the nudge, both while providing their information (often in a web survey) and after in a personal email.

4. *Offer an Embeddable Tool/Widget with Unique Functionality*

Flickr, Vimeo, Statcounter, Addthis, and Slideshare are all among the most linked-to sites on the web thanks to their popular embeddable widgets. Twitter, LinkedIn, Etsy, and Facebook all do likewise, employing snippets of code that can be placed on any web page and display information or provide functionality that a site owner couldn't on their own. And any site can build an embeddable widget—the key is to find something that other sites will have an incentive to share, build the widget such that links point back to the relevant pages, and spread the word (often through internal product usage). Embeddable content is a great way to not only earn links, but control what they say as they're linking back.

5. *Use Research Data in Commercial Content (and Inform the Researchers)*

The web offers a wealth of research from academic, corporate, and government sources, but these are frequently buried in hard-to-navigate sites inside tough-to-follow documents. By exposing research content in a more marketable, user-friendly way (think graphics, illustrations, videos, even simple, easy-to-read blog posts), you can add tremendous value to your niche's understanding of a topic and earn great links in return. One of my favorite tactics here is to contact those responsible for the research, let them know of your plans to use it, and invite them to help share the work. Many universities and research sites are thrilled to see others using their data and will happily link to it once live.

JOOST DE VALK

Joost de Valk is a well-known specialist in the fields of SEO and WordPress and web development, and often speaks on those topics at conferences like Search Engine Strategies, Search Marketing Expo, SASCon, A4UExpo, and WordCamps in various countries.

Joost is the founder and CEO of Yoast (www.yoast.com), which focuses on consulting in SEO, WordPress optimization, and online marketing and content strategy. Current clients include eBay, Facebook, RTL, Salesforce, and the European Patent Office. Before he founded Yoast, he worked at several online marketing agencies, advising companies like Conrad, KLM, Wegener, VNU, and *het Financieel Dagblad* (the Dutch *Financial Times*).

In addition to his work as an SEO consultant, public speaker, and developer, Joost has built many a plugin for WordPress (with more than 3.5 million downloads) and Firefox. He hosts the weekly WordPress Podcast and blogs on WordPress and SEO.

Joost talks on the topic of SEO, blogging, search marketing (SEO in advertising), and viral and social media marketing. In his presentations he shows, using many examples, how each online and offline company would benefit from search engine optimization and that no company can live without it.

Author Highlighting in Search Result Links by Joost de Valk

When you're trying to improve the authority of your site, you work on promoting yourself and your company as an authority everywhere. A big part of that is actually closer to another form of marketing: branding. The bigger brand you become in the hearts and minds of people who could potentially write about and link to your product(s), the bigger your chance of getting the kinds of links you want.

This means that when people are researching an article or blog post, they will often do a search, even when they already know you. When you rank there and they click through to you, you'll have strengthened your brand in their mind.

With the advent of Google+, Google has taken a few steps to help you cash in on your existing branding even more. When you search for a link-building expert, you'll quickly find Eric Ward. You will not find him with just some boring text result, but with an image and a reference to Eric's Google+ profile. If you already know him, you'll probably now click on.

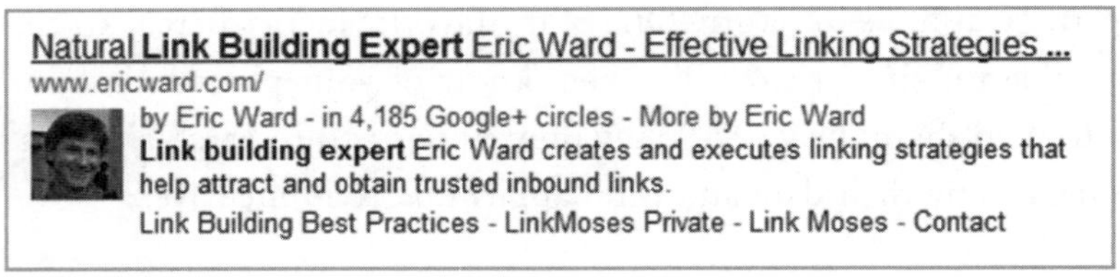

FIGURE 24–2. Implementing Author Highlighting Adds a Photo to Your Search Result

The implementation of this author highlight to the search snippet can be done in several ways, most of which are cumbersome, but one is relatively easy. Add a <link> tag in the <head> section of the pages you want so-called author highlights for and link those to your Google+ page. That's as simple as this, using myself as an example:

<link rel="author" href="https://plus.google.com/115369062315673853712/posts"/>

If you're lucky enough to be using WordPress, this is very easily done [using Joost's WordPress SEO plugin] as all you have to do is add your Google+ profile link on your WordPress profile page and it'll add it to all your posts and pages automatically.

There are two other things you need to check: Make sure the name you use on your site is 100 percent identical to what you use on Google+ and make sure your +1's on Google+ are public.

More on Snippet Optimization

While you're working on that "snippet," there's more you can do to increase the clicks you'll get from those rankings. Good link building will get you prime real estate in the search results. Once you've got it, it's up to you to make the most of that real estate.

A "regular" search result snippet already has several sections you can influence:

- The title
- The description
- The URL

The title has a big influence on search rankings, so you'll want to make sure your primary keyword is in there. At the same time you also want to make sure that title, which is the first thing people will read from you, entices them to click. The next bit they'll read is usually the description just below. As you could see in the example in Figure 24–2, Eric has taken the time to carefully craft a meta description that would help people understand what to expect.

The URL should, if possible, also contain your primary keyword, as it will give you another bit of bold in the search results, making your result stand out more. The goal of snippet optimization is simple: Get more relevant clicks by optimizing those three variables. Just improving relevant traffic is important: You don't want to drag people in with false promises. Doing that would increase your bounce rate, which, in the long run, only damages your site.

A great way to optimize your snippets is by using SEOmofo's Snippet Optimization Tool. Or, again if you're using WordPress, you could do this by using my WordPress SEO plugin, which shows this snippet preview straight on your edit page.

MIKE GREHAN

Mike Grehan is publisher of Search Engine Watch and ClickZ and producer of the SES international conference series. He is the current president of global trade association SEMPO, having been elected to the board of directors in 2010. Formerly, Mike worked as a search-marketing consultant with a number of international agencies, handling such global clients as SAP and Motorola. Recognized as a leading search-marketing expert, Mike came online in 1995 and is author of numerous books and white papers on the subject. His website is www.mikegrehan.com.

One of the most influential books in the history of web linking was written by the esteemed Mike Grehan, who also wrote the foreword for this book. Among the many remarkable aspects to this book is just how relevant it remains so many years after it was first written. The book has never been published anywhere other than as an electronic version produced by Mike himself. Here, with Mike's generous permission, for the first time is the entirety; please enjoy.

Filthy Linking Rich and Getting Richer! by Mike Grehan

As a kid, I once asked my father: How do you become a multimillionaire? He looked at me and said: "Easy! First you make a million . . ." and then he had a good laugh.

Come the latter part of the '60s, my father was a very wealthy man. As a serial entrepreneur, his interests in show business had netted him a fortune. He had opened his first nightclub in 1962, which was home to a local group called The Animals, who he helped on their way to international stardom (the bass player of the band and his former business partner would go on to manage Jimi Hendrix).

He drove a Jensen Interceptor (very cool car at the time), wore the most "fab gear" (Beatle-speak for hip clothes), and hung around Las Vegas with his pals quite a lot (a little too much for my mother's liking, unfortunately!). He was at the peak of his career and a major influencer within his social group. Not bad for a guy who had to catapult himself from his early beginnings as a typewriter salesman.

It was some time later in life when my father and I were talking about wealth creation that he used the expression: The rich get richer.

I'll come back to my dear departed Dad again, but stay with me right now, as this is going somewhere. And I'm afraid some of it may be pretty bleak reading if you have newly created, lowly indexed web pages and you're desperately waiting for someone to link to them so that they stand a chance of ranking in a search engine with a static link-based algorithm.

I have to tell you, for the past 18 months, I've been absorbed in an entirely new world of research. Network science can be regarded as a branch of complexity theory. Complexity itself describes any number of different sciences, theories, and world views such as chaos theory, emergence, and network science. And it's fascinating. In fact, I'll go as far as saying enthralling.

By trying to further increase my understanding of the real power of linkage data in search engine algorithms (to be shared with you in the upcoming third edition of my book), I've become even more aware of how "the rich get richer" power law affects search engine results and also the ecology of the web itself. The richer you are with links pointing back to your site, the richer you are likely to become in search marketing terms.

Are search engines giving a fair representation of what's actually available on the web? Not really. If pages were judged on the quality and the relevance for ranking, then there would be less search engine bias toward pages that are simply popular by "linkage voting." Unfortunately, quality is subjective, so finding a universally acceptable measurement or metric is not going to be easy.

If you're involved in the search marketing industry, particularly on the link-building side, then you'll know better than most that getting links for a large and more visible website is easier than getting links for a startup or a mom-and-pop-type outfit.

Now you may feel that you're about to read something obvious and decide to skip the rest here. But please stay with me a little longer.

I believe you may be very interested to know that the scale of the problem is rapidly getting greater with the bias of a static-based "link popularity" algorithm such as PageRank, largely the cause of the problem.

"Now wait a minute, Grehan," I hear you say. "Aren't you the biggest skeptic about PageRank and its role in Google search results?" And the answer is, "You bet I am." However, what I want to do with this feature article is to . . . highlight how great the bias is for high-ranking pages, which are fundamentally ordered on link based-algorithms to attract more links. And why I believe (along with many in the research community) it's becoming necessary for search engines to seek a new paradigm. I think it is of benefit to the search marketing community as a whole to understand the implications of such concerns by search engines to move away from current methodology as it will certainly have its impact on our industry.

When speaking on the subject of linking at conferences, seminars, and workshops, I always attempt to explain the different manner in which search engine marketers look at links on the web compared to the way search engines view the same data. Search engine marketers are concerned, basically, with a hyperlink from another page back to theirs. And generally speaking, the more the merrier!

However, search engines take a much more mathematical, philosophical, and analytical impression of the entire web (or more to the point, the fraction of it that they have captured). To search engines, web pages that are linked together are nodes in the web graph. By applying random graph theory to the web, they have viewed it as a type of static, equilibrium network with a classic, Poisson-type distribution of connections.

Even though graph theory has made great progress and been an important factor in the way that search engines have been able to plot crawling of the web and ranking of documents, we now know that the most important natural and artificial networks have a specific architecture based on a fat-tailed distribution of the number of connections of vertices that differs crucially from the classical random graphs studied by mathematicians. Because, as a rule, these networks are not static but evolving objects.

It's really only been the last five years or so that physicists have started extensive empirical and theoretical research into networks that are organized this way. The main focus prior to this research was in neural and Boolean networks, where the arrangements of connections was secondary.

So now I hear you say: "Hey, Mike... Whoa! Stick with search engines and optimization and suchlike. I'm a search engine marketer, not a physicist! Random graph theory, equilibrium network with a classic Poisson-type distribution, fat-tailed distribution, neural networks... I'm brain zonked already and this is only the second page of your article."

Yup, I understand that, I've scrambled my own brains a bit a few times recently. But it's important that you do know a little more about what's really going on in the research field to provide a better analysis of what currently makes one web page more important than another and how that is likely to change.

Your business may depend greatly on being able to optimize for search engines. And that's only going to become harder and harder.

Tell you what I'll do—I'll back up a bit here and try and do a brief history to what I've been kind of "glossing over."

Let's have a slightly (and I do mean slightly) more in-depth look at network science and how it is mathematically, philosophically, and otherwise applied to search. As Russian physicist and genius Sergei Dorogovstev put it in his excellent text, *Evolution of Networks*, from last year, I feel it's "more important to be understood than to be perfectly rigorous." Although I have tried to eliminate the math as best as I can and stick to the principles, there are bound to be sections which do reference formula. Therefore, brave reader, as I frequently do myself, don't be afraid to skim over some parts you don't understand to reach those that you do. Remember: Like you, I'm a search engine marketer—not a scientist.

The history behind social network concepts and graph theory applied to ranking algorithms is something that can help you understand a lot more about their complexities and why some of your best SEO endeavors may, already, not be working.

It may seem as if the web grows in a very unorganized and haphazard way. But that's not really the case. It's beginning to show powerful underlying regularities from the way in which web pages link together to the patterns found in the way users browse.

And it's interesting to note that these regularities have been predicted on the basis of theoretical models from a field of physics, statistical mechanics, that few would have thought would apply to the web.

Among the chaos of activity and information on the web, scientists have analyzed data that has been collected by the internet archive and other sources, which has helped to uncover hidden patterns that hold many clues to what's really happening in cyberspace.

These patterns are being discovered all the more by the many researchers worldwide who are intrigued by the new science of networks. And the discoveries they make are both surprising and very, very interesting.

What is of most interest to us in our little search-marketing community is how quickly researchers have established that the distribution of pages and links per website follows a universal and lawful behavior. The simple truth of the matter is, few sites have enormous numbers of pages and many have few. And it follows that few sites have many links pointing to them whereas many have few.

How is it that the web in its distribution follows some kind of known patterns, when there is no central planner of the web? There is no central body to suggest how it should grow and who should have links and who should not.

You need to look at the origins of network theory that throw a light on a number of social mechanisms which operate beyond the world wide web. These theories help to explain why the web has become a huge informational ecosystem that can be used to quantitatively measure and test theories of human behavior and social interaction.

Phrases such as "it's a small world" and "the rich get richer" and "well-connected" have worked their way into everyday vocabulary. It's interesting that such phrases have been the byproduct of a mixture of research in social network analysis, physics, mathematics, and computer science, all of which can (and do) apply to the algorithms used by the major search engines.

It's a Small World

In the 1960s, American psychologist Stanley Milgram was intrigued by the composition of the web of interpersonal connections that link people into a community. To inform himself more about this, he sent letters to a random selection of people living in Nebraska and Kansas, asking them, in turn, to forward the letters to a stockbroker in Boston. But he didn't give them the address of the stockbroker. Instead he asked them to forward the letter only to someone they knew personally and whom they thought may be "socially" closer to the stockbroker.

Most of the letters did, in fact, eventually make it to the stockbroker. But the much more startling fact was how quickly they did so. It wasn't a case of hundreds of mailings to reach the final target, but typically, just six or so.

This true experiment has passed into folklore and is now famously known as "six degrees of separation," although it wasn't Milgram who named it so; that was from the 1993 play of the same name:

"I read somewhere that everybody on this planet is separated by only six other people. Six degrees of separation between us and everyone else on this planet."

—Ouisa Kitteridge, from John Guare's play, *Six Degrees of Separation*

Popular culture plays its part again, when in 1997, a new game called "The Kevin Bacon Game" arrived on the scene. The game was invented by a couple of movie buffs who (for some reason of their own) had come to the conclusion that Kevin Bacon was the true center of the movie universe (it has been proven that he is actually *not* the most connected actor in Hollywood circles, but nevertheless . . .).

If you haven't heard of the game, here's how it works. The movie network consists of actors who are connected by virtue of the fact that they have acted together in one or more feature films.

And this is not just Hollywood. This is any movie made anywhere. According to the Internet Movie Database (IMDB), between the years 1898 and 2000, roughly half a million people have acted in more than 200,000 feature films.

So, here we go . . . If you have acted in a movie with Kevin Bacon, then you have a Bacon number of one (Bacon himself has a Bacon number of 0). As Bacon has acted in more than 50 movies, he has acted with more than 1,150 other actors. It follows, therefore, that more than 1,150 actors have a Bacon number of one. Moving outward from Bacon, if you ever acted with an actor who had appeared with Bacon, then you have a Bacon number of two. And so on and so forth...

But the Kevin Bacon game is not the only one in town.

It's actually based on "Erdos numbers," these being applied to the distance between mathematicians who wrote a paper with the great Paul Erdos (we're coming to him in more detail in just a few paragraphs) and those who authored a paper with a person who authored a paper with Erdos, and so on and so forth.

Much like the Kevin Bacon game, the smaller your "Erdos number" the higher the prestige you have within the mathematician community.

The existence of these short chains of acquaintance have actually been observed and documented by social network scientists for years.

Milgram's experiment with the Boston stockbroker raised a couple of interesting issues, one regarding the properties that networks must have to become small worlds. If you were to draw a network of people (nodes) and links between those nodes relating to who knows whom, it wouldn't be at all obvious that any two nodes would be separated by six links. This is because there is something peculiar about a social network that is reflected in its link structure.

The second issue concerns what the best strategies are for navigating such small-world graphs in a short number of steps. Think about the people in Milgram's experiment. They did not have detailed knowledge of the social network in which they were embedded, but they still managed to pass the messages in a fairly short number of links.

These issues have since been addressed by Duncan Watts and Steven Strogatz at Cornell University and also Jon Kleinberg (in a small world way) also at Cornell. However, the conclusions and finding are vastly beyond the scope of this paper as an introduction and covered in more detail in the third edition of my book.

Does the same small-world phenomenon exist between websites and web pages? A few years ago, Lada Adamic, of Xerox, Palo Alto Research Center, undertook a study of the average number of links you would need to traverse to get from one site on the web to another. She discovered that, just as in the social sphere, one could pick two sites at random and get from one to the other within four clicks.

This phenomenon was again shown to exist for the number of links between any two pages on the web. Albert-Lazlo Barabasi, at Notre Dame University (more about Barabasi coming) discovered that, in the case of pages, the number is 19.

Getting Connected

Hungarian mathematician and genius Paul Erdos was the first to address the fundamental question pertaining to our understanding of an interconnected universe: How do networks form? His solutions laid the foundations of the theory of random networks. To explain: Suppose we take a collection of dots on a page and then just haphazardly wire them together—the result is what mathematicians refer to as a random graph.

Okay, now imagine that you've been given the task of building roads to connect up the towns of an undeveloped country. At this time, there are no roads at all, just 50 isolated towns scattered across the map. Because the construction guys are likely to misunderstand your plans and build roads linking the wrong towns and, of course, the country has so little money, you need to build as few roads as possible. The question is then: How many will be enough?

Mathematician and author Mark Buchanan, in his excellent book *Nexus,* explained it this way:

If finance wasn't a problem, then you'd simply order the construction guys to keep building until every last pair of towns were linked together. To link each of the 50 towns to all 49 others would take 1,225 roads. But what is the smallest number of roads you need to build to be reasonably sure that drivers can go between any two towns without ever leaving a road?

It's one of the most famous problems in graph theory and could be expressed in any number of ways; houses and telephone links, the power grid, etc. It's a very difficult problem to solve and took the considerable mind power of Erdos back in 1959.

In this particular problem, it turns out that the random placement of 98 roads is adequate to make sure that the towns are connected. Even if that seems like a lot of roads, it actually only represents 8 percent of the original figure of 1,225 roads in total.

Erdos discovered that, no matter how many points there might be, a small percentage of randomly placed links is always enough to tie the network together into a more or less completely connected whole. To put this into the internet perspective, the percentage required dwindles as the network gets bigger. For a network of 300 points, there are nearly 50,000 possible links that could run between them.

But if no more than 2 percent of these are in place, the network will be completely connected. For 1,000 points, the crucial factor is less than 1 percent. And for 10 million points, it is only 0.00000166.

So, does that mean that if people were linked more or less at random, the typical person would have to know only about one out of every 250 million for the entire population of the world to be linked into a social web?

Let me just make a note here: One of the primary features of a random graph is that its degree distribution always has a particular mathematical form known as Poisson distribution (named in honor of the French mathematician).

The Rich Get Richer

I want to just skip forward very quickly here for a moment. By 1999, Hungarian physicist Albert-Lazlo Barabasi had become completely engrossed in network theory; in particular, its application to the web. He himself had been schooled in the Hungarian tradition of graph theory, including the Erdos model of random graphs.

His excellent work in the field has given great insight into networks as diverse as those that begin as cocktail parties right up to the growth of the national power grid.

And his innovative work has shown that many networks in the real world have degree distributions that don't look anything like a Poisson distribution. Instead, they follow what is known as a power law.

Barabasi's body of work has transformed the study of links and nodes. He has discovered that all networks have a deep underlying order and operate according to simple but powerful rules.

Duncan J. Watts, one of the principal architects of network theory, has argued that the origin of the Poisson degree in a random graph, and its corresponding cutoff, lies with its most basic premise: that links between nodes come into existence entirely independently of one another.

This means that, in an egalitarian system, things average out over time. An individual node can be unlucky for a while, but eventually, it has to be on the receiving end of a new connection. And in the same way, no run of luck can go on forever, so if one node gets picked up more frequently than average for some period of time, eventually others will catch up.

But you know, real life is not that fair, unfortunately. Particularly when it comes to matters of wealth and success. Let's just think about the growth of a social web, as posed earlier, from the mathematician's viewpoint to begin with.

Duncan Watts puts it this way. Imagine you have a hundred friends. And each one of those also has a hundred friends. This means that at one degree of separation you can connect to 100 people and within two degrees you can reach 100 times 100, which is 10,000 people. By three degrees, you are up to almost one million; by four, nearly a hundred million; and in five degrees about 9 billion people. What this would mean is that if everyone in the world had one hundred friends, then within six steps, you can easily connect yourself to the population of the entire planet.

But as he also points out, if you're at all socially inclined, you'll already have spotted the fatal flaw in the reasoning.

A hundred friends is a lot to think about. So think about your ten best friends and then ask yourself who their ten best friends are. And the chances are that you'll come up with many of the same people. Go to Orkut now (if you can remember what Orkut is!) and check on your ten best pals in the search marketing network to get a real-life understanding of this.

It's what's known as clustering. We tend not so much to have friends as we do groups of friends, based on shared interests, experience, and location, all of which overlap with other groups. And this is an almost universal feature, not just of social networks, but of networks in general.

It's this social network phenomenon that is the underlying cause of the rich getting richer. And this phenomenon has been with us for a long, long time. The great

20th-century sociologist Robert Merton dubbed it the "Matthew effect" as a reference to a passage in the Bible, in which Matthew observes, "For unto everyone that hath shall be given, and he shall have abundance; but from him that hath not shall be taken away even that which he hath."

(Once the vision of Michael Palin, in Monty Python's *Life of Brian,* dissipates from your mind, I'll continue here . . .)

The Matthew effect, when applied to networks, basically equates to well-connected nodes being more likely to attract new links, while poorly connected nodes are disproportionately likely to remain poor.

In fact, it has been proposed that "the rich get richer" effect drives the evolution of real networks. If one node has twice as many links as another node, then it is precisely twice as likely to receive a new link.

Let's return, for a moment, to Barabasi's introduction of power laws to bring us into a real-world example. The distribution of wealth in the United States, for instance, resembles a power law. The 19th-century Parisian engineer Vilifredo Pareto was the first to notice this phenomenon, which subsequently became known as Pareto's law and demonstrated that it held true in every European country for which the relevant statistics existed.

The law shows that very many people possess very little wealth, while a very small minority are extremely wealthy. We tend to refer to Pareto's law more generally as the 80/20 principle.

Interestingly, a similar process tends to underlie the growth of social networks. A study by sociologists Fredrick Liljeros and Christopher Edling of Stockholm University, working with a team of physicists from Boston University, looked at the links of the sexual contact between 2,810 randomly selected individuals in Sweden. If acquaintance is a fairly loosely defined relationship, the existence of, or nonexistence of, a sexual link is not.

In the sexual context, these are the people who Malcolm Gladwell, in his book *The Tipping Point*, referred to as "the connectors"—a socially prolific few who tie an entire social network together.

You might put the prolific performance of the connectors in a sexual-contact network down to special skills given at birth, or in early childhood.

But in the experiment carried out by Liljeros, another plausible explanation for the structure of the sexual contact network includes the increased skill in acquiring new partners, as the number of previous partners grows, and the motivation to have many new partners simply to sustain self-image.

As you can see, it's evident in the sexual-contact network that "the rich get richer" here, too.

This is a scale-free network described by Albert-Lazlo Barabasi as a power-law or fat-tail distribution for network elements according to the number of links they have.

The physicists themselves believe that their approach is the best for understanding the evolution of networks. It's a direct generalization of the usual physics of growth, percolation phenomena, diffusion, self-organized criticality, mesoscopic systems, etc.

The physicists' approach has brought with it enough mathematical and computational data that you can fry your brains just trying to get your head around the basic concepts. But that's not what I'm trying to achieve here. I'm hoping that I'm able to give some basic but useful background to the way that social network concepts are applied and identified in the connectivity graphs used by each search engine when analyzing linkage data. You should also note, of course, that "connectionism" is very much a descriptive word applied to the field of AI.

Perhaps the greatest discovery of the laws of network organization focuses on the idea of "hubs" and how they form. These are the centerpieces of networks, around which many links form.

Before we even apply it to the web and search, a strong case has been made by Barabasi (and subsequently by others) that the best way to combat AIDS, for instance, would be to concentrate on identifying and treating the hubs in sexual contact networks.

Information about the structure of the web is of great importance to search engines. The common observation is that one good web document tends to link to other good documents of similar content. Therefore there will be groups of pages of similar content (and similar quality) that refer to each other. The quality of the pages is presumed to be guaranteed by the recommendations implicit in the links between them. However, as we shall discover, this is not necessarily a good metric overall for quality as many had first thought.

Lada Adamic (Xerox) tested her theories (mentioned earlier) built around an application to examine a repository of web pages crawled by Google. For any given search word, she brought back results to the queries which provided PageRank, text match, and link information for each page.

She then identified all the connected clusters and selected the largest one, as it would most likely contain links across sites other than just the common ones. What she discovered was connected clusters spanning several sites tend to contain the main relevant pages and are rich in "hubs" (pages which contain links to many other good pages). It is then possible to find the center of the cluster by computing the number of links among all the members of the cluster.

This shows that, rather than presenting a list of documents that contain many sequential entries from the same site, a search engine, using the phenomenon of the "small world," can present just the center from each cluster. Users can then explore the rest of the cluster on their own.

Hyperlink-Based "Popularity" Algorithms

Maybe it was a small-world event in a scale-free network (pun), or simply a quirk of fate that Jon Kleinberg, foremost computer scientist, found himself as a professor at Cornell University at just the same time as foremost physicist and sociologist Duncan Watts. Whatever it was, the information exchange between them in the study of networks has helped to transform the way that search engines relied almost solely on methods such as the vector space model which had pages "standing in isolation" to the two major hyperlink analysis algorithms: Hits and PageRank.

The application of network analysis and physics has given search engines fundamental principles to base ranking mechanisms on, among other things, clustering, interconnectivity, and popularity.

I don't need to tell you that the majority of web page accesses are referred by search engines; you already know this. Given the sheer quantity of information on the web, it's no wonder that search engines have become an indispensable tool.

An individual could never sift through the billions of pages online trying to find the ten best. So, that becomes the job of the search engine: to narrow it down to a smaller number of pages worth looking at.

This method of "topic distillation" to tackle the issue of the "abundance problem," i.e., too many relevant pages being returned for a query, with little indication as to which are the most important, or authoritative, is centered around PageRank and Hits.

These algorithms applied to the link structure of the web fundamentally suggest the higher number of quality links you have pointing back at you, the higher you should rank in the results. It's a popularity metric.

Of course, the fact that strong hubs form in networks such as the web, the utopian dream of a free and equally democratic internet that many have dreamed of, becomes somewhat nonsense. Having covered the basic ideas of how networks form and strengthen and dominate topological degrees gives us an indication of what is bound to follow with a static hyperlink-based ranking algorithm.

I write a lot about hits/clever, which is a query-specific algorithm. Using this approach, hits builds a subgraph of the web that is relevant to the query and then uses link analysis to rank the pages of the subgraph. But [here] I just want to stick with PageRank, as it is this approach that causes the accelerating "rich get richer" problem that many search marketers struggle with.

PageRank is the most visible of the link-based algorithms due to its association with Google, and can be referred to more as a static ranking scheme. Using this method, all pages to be indexed are ordered once and for all in a best-to-worst rank, regardless of any query. When the query does arrive, the index returns the best ten pages that satisfy the query at the top of the pile. Best, here, being determined by the static ranking.

But this is also the creator of a very worrisome problem that affects new web pages with low linkage data, regardless of the quality of those pages. Quality and relevance are sometimes at odds with each other. And the ecology of the web may be suffering because of the way search engines are biased toward a page's popularity more than its quality. In short, "currently popular" pages are repeatedly being returned at the top of the results at the major search engines.

So, the "filthy linking rich" get richer and currently popular pages continue to hit the top spots. The law of "preferential attachment," as it is also known, wherein new links on the web are more likely to go to sites that already have many links, proves that the scheme is inherently biased against new and unknown pages.

When search engines constantly return popular pages at the top of the pile, more web users discover those pages and more web users are likely to link to them. This therefore means that currently unpopular pages (as such) are not returned by search engines (regardless of quality) so they are discovered by very few web users. And this, of course, is unfortunate for both the publishers of web pages and the seekers of their information. (Not to mention web marketers!)

This has been a lengthy journey already and we're still only scratching the surface. I want to finish by making you aware of an experiment that took place in America.

First of all, the experiment suggested that by 2002, around 70 percent of all web searches online were being handled by Google. They also suggested that while Google takes into account more than 100 factors in its ranking algorithm, the core of it is based on PageRank. This is a "static" link popularity metric to represent importance or authority for ranking purposes.

Now it's important to understand that there is a distinction between the importance or quality of a page to that of the relevance of a page following a user query.

The scientists suggest that the relevance is a quantity that relies heavily on the particular search issued by the user. But the importance or quality of a document could actually be computed at crawl time and could be seen as intrinsic to the document itself.

And the reason they are looking at this intrinsic quality is based on the desire to find a new paradigm for ranking web pages that is not so heavily based on link popularity, the problem being that Google repeatedly returns "currently popular" pages at the top of the results and ignores newer pages that are not so densely connected. Therefore it is inherently biased against "unknown" pages.

So are the "rich getting richer" insofar as linkage is concerned at search engines? Yes, and it's a rapidly worsening factor. The experiment carried out covered data collected over a seven-month period. And from that experimental data, they observed that the top 20 percent of the pages with the highest number of incoming links obtained 70 percent of the new links after seven months, while the bottom 60 percent of the pages obtained virtually no incoming links at all during that period.

So where's the good news, Mike? Well, there is a little consolation in that the "rich get richer" behavior varies in different categories. A new model has been developed which can be used to predict and analyze competition and diversity in different communities on the web.

However, that is covered in more detail again in the third edition of *Search Engine Marketing: The Essential Best Practice Guide.*

I'll round up here where I started with my dear departed Dad. Just as he became a social bright light earning (and burning) lots of cash, so he attracted lots of new friends (links). But when the Gaming and Lotteries Act in the late '60s forced him to close many of his venues (something he hadn't seen coming), the cash reserves slipped away, and so did the friends.

Still, he left me with one excellent piece of advice. I said to him, "It's all right saying you become a multimillionaire by becoming a millionaire first, but how do you do that?"

He looked and smiled and said, "In my experience, I've discovered that looking for the million-dollar deal is very difficult. Getting a million dollars from one person is hard. However, getting one dollar from a million people is really not so difficult."

Like myself, my father was much more of an optimist than a physicist!

Chapter 25

Link-Building Strategies
A Quick Reference for Brainstorming
by Jon Cooper, http://pointblankseo.com

Whether you bookmark or dog-ear this page, make sure it's easily accessible. This chapter acts as a reference for almost every link-building strategy known to man. If you ever run out of ideas or hit a wall, this is where you should turn.

Note: I've tried to give examples on as many as possible. Some sections are littered with examples, while others were too difficult to find.

BASIC STRATEGIES
Create a Blog

Creating content on a consistent basis not only builds links internally (by linking out from your posts), but also gives you the ability to build links naturally, because content is your greatest asset when attracting links. A blog is essential to many strategies we'll outline here, such as linking out. You absolutely need a blog in today's online environment to survive.

Internal Linking

You have pages and posts on your website, so make the most of them. Internal links are huge for link building because you can control everything about them, from the location on the page to the anchor text.

This is something that most people overlook—please do not! Make sure to steer your content in the direction of other posts or pages so you can link to them.

Warning: Do not use exact-match anchor text in your site's navigation (sitewide links). This will most likely be another spam filter from Google.

Resources/Links Pages

Other webmasters have created links, or resource, pages, and these are legitimate opportunities to get links. If the links on that page are relevant, you've got a chance.

Unfortunately, it's not as easy as just asking for a link. The following are specific strategies to help you get webmasters liking you before you ask, and greatly increase your chance of getting the link.

Ask People You Know for a Link

Whether it's your friends, relatives, employees, colleagues, business partners, clients, or anyone else, ask them for a link. Someone you know has a website or blog, so take advantage.

Make It Easy to Link to You

If you want people to link to you, make it easy for them. Create HTML-ready snippets that people can plug right into their content to link to you, because some linkers in your community might not be too web-savvy. Either create a "Link to Us" page or use a little JavaScript to generate the HTML at the end of each article or post.

Note: This might not be the best option for every community. Are you in the cement niche? Then this is perfect. Are you talking about internet-related business? Then this might not be your best bet, because the majority of your audience probably already knows how to link.

Research Competitors

When it comes to finding new link opportunities, competitor research is one of the first things you should do. Essentially, you're piggy-backing off of their success. While some links are unobtainable (i.e., a random mention in a news post), others can be diamonds in the rough (a high-quality niche directory).

I suggest using SEOmoz's Open Site Explorer for this. Plugin your competitors and export their backlinks to a CSV file. Do this for all your competitors so you can get all of their links in one place in a spreadsheet workbook. Then you can sort them by various link metrics to find the best opportunities.

Link Out

Linking out is huge. Don't be a link hoarder; you're going to create content, so use it to gain favor with other people. I'll go more in depth below with specific strategies on linking out.

Build Relationships

This is the #1 link-building strategy in the world. Get to know people! Build relationships with them, because it'll come back to you in the form of links (that is, if they're the *right* people).

The best part about this is that it's just like real life. Remember how people say, "It's not about what you know, it's about who you know"? The same goes for link building.

Niche-Specific Directories

As opposed to general web directories, niche-specific directories only accept sites that meet a certain topic criteria. For example, one directory might only accept sites about arts and crafts. Some of these directories are free, while others are paid. One example is Business.com, a directory for business websites. Cost is $299/year.

Paid Directories

Some directories ask for money before accepting your link(s) in their listings. Once again, while some of these can pass legitimate value, others pass little and aren't worth your time or money. For example, Dir.Yahoo.com is a paid directory.

CONTENT-BASED LINK-BUILDING STRATEGIES

You can use your content to build links. Most of these strategies don't necessarily attract links, but they can if the content is good enough.

Guest Posting

Bloggers sometimes have trouble cranking out content on a regular basis. That's where you can help. Pitch bloggers to ask if you could guest blog, because if they say yes, you can get a few links from the post, and if the blog is popular, you can drive a bit of traffic to your site, too.

If you want, use sites like BloggerLinkUp.com and MyBlogGuest.com to connect with bloggers who need content. It's scalable, but the bloggers you get in touch with aren't usually very authoritative (they're mostly mid-level bloggers).

Educational Content

If you're trying to get links from colleges, create content targeted at them that you can use during outreach. There's usually something you know that you could write an entire tutorial on that would interest college webmasters.

> **TIP**
>
> Seek out pages on .edu websites that feature similar content, then do any of the strategies listed under "Helping Webmasters" on page 207 to help get on their good side.

Green Content

Just like educational content, create something that targets a specific community (in this case, environmentalists). They've got hoards of link juice just waiting to be tapped into.

Simply outreaching to green bloggers and letting them know about your content usually does the trick. If the content is good enough, and if it's a complete conversation (i.e., a huge infographic on the environmental impact of drift nets), they'll usually dedicate an entire post to it.

> **TIP**
>
> An infographic or something similar would work great, because all a community has to do is embed it in their content. If there's any community willing to embed an info-graphic that's *relevant and worth sharing*, it's the green community.

Images

Something so frequently overlooked is the use of images for link building. Bloggers just like me struggle to find images relevant to our content, so why not take advantage? When people use your images you'll get an attribution link in return (that's if they're honest).

A great idea is to always have a camera with you whenever you're at an industry event. Imagine if you took 100 pictures at PubCon of all the different speakers and published them on a certain portion of your site.

TIP

Hotlink your images (see: pointblankseo.com/book/hotlink). Make it easy for publishers to copy and paste HTML code right into their posts. This not only makes it easier to use your images, it also makes it much more likely you'll get a link from each.

Free Charts/Graphs

If you've got a few tidbits of data lying around, make them into charts and graphs. Just like images, you'll get attribution links.

For example, look at SEOmoz's free charts: SEOmoz.org/dp/free-charts.

Writing Testimonials

Right now, list any services or products you've bought recently. As long as it's not a product or service from a massive company (i.e., Walmart), there's a good chance you can get a link in exchange for a testimonial. You can find writing testimonials at StartLogic. com/startlogic/testimonials.bml.

Get Interviewed

Just like you should interview others, seize opportunities to be interviewed, no matter how small the audience is. The 5 to 600 words that take you 15 to 20 minutes can turn into a few highly authoritative, contextual links.

Contribute to crowdsourced posts—just like with interviews, if someone reaches out to you to participate in a crowdsourced post, make sure you contribute. The questions usually don't take more than five to ten minutes of your time, and you'll get a decent link or two from it.

LINK ATTRACTION

Outreach and submissions only go so far. Sometimes you have to let your content attract links naturally to get the results you want.

If you create content that naturally attracts links, it not only saves you time getting them manually, but it also increases engagement on your blog (if it's worth linking to, it's usually worth reading). This is where your content and link-building strategies meet.

Ego Bait

It's a fact of life: People like to look good. If you're featured as one of the top bloggers in your niche, you're probably going to spread the word. By appealing to the egos of people, companies, and communities, they'll help spread the word about your content.

For example, I wrote a post that appealed to some of the authorities in the SEO industry, who all helped me spread the word, and you can read it at: pointblankseo.com/book/ego.

Contrary Hook

If there's controversy in your industry, or if someone has one particular view on a topic, don't be afraid to write up a post on the opposing view. If you do it quick enough, and enough people agree with you, you could attract links from your supporters like there's no tomorrow.

But if the greater community doesn't accept your view, don't let that stop you from voicing your opinion. This could actually work in your favor, because when opposers write on the topic, they'll probably link to you as to what they don't agree with when they make their case.

For example, this post by Rand Fishkin in response to Kris Roadruck's post (pointblankseo.com/book/kris) attracted more than 1,000 links from over 180 root domains: pointblankseo.com/book/rand.

Live Blogging

If you're at an industry event, blog about everything that's taking place. If you're the only one, you'll get loads of links. If you're not, you'll still get a lot of attention.

Yes, the following is Wired.com, so it's a little unfair, but hopefully you can learn how it's done from this example online: pointblankseo.com/book/live (451 links from 140 root domains in three months).

How-Tos and Tutorials

Whether it's a tool, DIY project, or anything else, showing people exactly how to do something is extremely helpful.

For example, this RSS tutorial (mnot.net/rss/tutorial) attracted more than 8,000 links from over 600 root domains.

Glossary of Terms

Newbies in your industry probably don't know all the jargon you and other bloggers are using. Do them a favor and create a glossary of industry terms and acronyms.

This glossary of internet terms (matisse.net/files/glossary.html) landed more than 2,600 links from over 1,200 root domains (imagine if you made an updated version!).

White Papers

You might be thinking research and white papers are the same, but they're not. Someone writing a research paper doesn't know what the outcome will be; someone writing a white paper has a clear understanding of the objectives and intended results from the beginning.

For example, you could outline an entire sector of an industry from top to bottom.

This one (bitcoin.org/bitcoin.pdf) outlined the company and its services and got more than 300 links from over 100 root domains. If a boring one like this could get links, imagine what you could do with more exciting content!

Quizzes/Tests

Testing your reader's knowledge and letting them share their results with their friends is always a great idea.

OKCupid's 2008 politics test (okcupid.com/politics) attracted more than 1,600 links from over 500 root domains.

Research Papers

Going all out and diving deep into a subject is a great way to establish yourself as an industry leader. It's also a great way to attract a few links. If you make any major discoveries, you'll get at least a few citations from scholarly and news websites.

For example, this paper, which attracted more than 7,600 links from more than 1,500 root domains, might look a little familiar: pointblankseo.com/book/paper.

Timely/Seasonal Content

Creating the right content at the right time can get you a ton of attention. Creating an infographic on the statistics behind this year's Super Bowl the day after the event is a perfect example.

The same goes for seasonal content. Whether it's Valentine's Day, Christmas, or Halloween, you can create holiday-themed content that can get a ton of attention over a short period of time (and every year after).

There aren't any link statistics of this at the time of this writing, but this is a great example from TurboTax: pointblankseo.com/book/timely.

Case Studies

Everyone loves a good case study. Real results with real numbers can instantly catch people's attention. If you offer a product or service, this is a no-brainer. If you give out advice, find someone who's used it successfully.

Although this particular case study didn't attract more than 200 links, it's still a great example of what one should look like: pointblankseo.com/book/case.

Humor

Creating a parody, spoof, or industry jokes list is a great way to loosen up your readers. People love sharing things they can laugh at.

The Onion, a fake news network, is built on humor. This story in particular attracted more than 4,400 links from 1,200 root domains: pointblankseo.com/book/onion. No, you're not a major site like *The Onion*, but making a similarly funny industry news story is something worth thinking about.

Printable Resources

People like hard copies of useful guides. By creating a printable resource with an awesome design, you can almost guarantee a few links will come your way.

For example, check out this case study about how Brian Flores created a printable HTML5 cheat sheet that got shared by the Google Developers G+ page: pointblankseo. com/book/printable.

Creating Contests

Entering contests is great for link building, but creating them is even better. By requiring your participants to write about and link to the contest from their blog, you'll not only get links from them, but their posts will increase the exposure of your contest, thus growing your number of contestants at an exponential rate (and thus, the amount of links you get).

I'd give you an example, but they're everywhere; contest creation isn't a secret.

Covering News First

This one's tough, but remember to always keep it in mind. If you see someone talking about a developing story, and no one has covered it yet, start mashing on your keyboard at lightning speed.

A good way to do this is by making sure all of the news sources are in your RSS feed reader. For example, if I wanted to cover the latest development of search engines, the Google, Yahoo, and Bing blogs would all be in my reader.

It's difficult to give an example for this because when it's all said and done, it's not easy finding the original story that covered the news first.

Infographics

People love data, but sometimes it's hard to digest. Creating an infographic on it is a popular way to change that. Not only will it naturally attract links, but you'll also get other bloggers embedding it, which means even more links! Not to mention you have control over the anchor text of the embed code.

Here's a fantastic case study on an infographic that not only netted a ton of links, but also some serious traffic and social traction: pointblankseo.com/book/infographics.

Web Tools

Creating free online tools, such as specialized calculators, is a fantastic way to attract links. They don't even have to be complex. If it could save me five minutes, then I'll probably use and share it.

A fantastic example of a simple, yet effective free online tool is this one by Solo SEO: pointblankseo.com/book/tool. I can't count how many times I've seen SEO bloggers like me link to it. It's netted almost 500 links from almost 200 root domains.

Interactive—Content Your User Can Alter, Change, or Remix

The next big thing in linkbait is interactive content. The reason: because it's flat out cool and few people are doing it.

You can see what Thomson.co.uk did with this at: pointblankseo.com/book/interactive.

Info-Animations

Instead of creating an infographic, why not create a video that displays the same information? It's a lot different than what most are doing, and that's a good thing. The best part is that it works the same way as infographics; the video can be embedded and can act as a post by itself. Check out this animation at: pointblankseo.com/book/animation.

Review Something New

Just like with news, if you're the first to review something, and if it's awesome, your review will get tons of attention.

You can also use this to gain favor with the creators of the product or service you're creating.

I reviewed Domain Hunter Plus, a new link checker, and not only did I get a few links to the review, but the creator of the tool worked out a deal with me by linking to the review and my homepage from the tool's homepage, which now has a PageRank of 5.

Utilize National Days and Events

Whether it's a national day, week, month, or event, they can all be used to build links. You could create your own, or you could help promote an existing one. If this is something you're serious about doing, then check out this post: pointblankseo.com/book/national.

Drawings

Using drawings to appeal to emotion can work great if it strikes the right tone with your audience.

This drawing attracted more than 15,000 links from more than 350 root domains: pointblankseo.com/book/drawing.

Webinars

Spending a couple of hours every month doing a webinar is a great idea for attracting links over the long term. Set up a page on your website solely dedicated to webinars, and as you create new ones, the links will roll in each time.

HubSpot has done a great job with this, having more than 1,000 links from 100 root domains to their Webinars page: hubspot.com/marketing-webinars.

Games

Creating exciting games to keep visitors content is not only a strategy to attract links to the game itself, but if you make it embeddable, other webmasters will put it on their sites (if it's good enough), which means even more links.

Travelpod made a "Traveler IQ Challenge" that's netted 7,800 links from almost 1,000 root domains: pointblankseo.com/book/game. Better yet, they made it embeddable!

Surveys

There's generally a two-step process to attracting links with surveys.

The first step is asking people to participate. If it's on a particularly interesting topic, reaching out to bloggers, experts, and industry news sites to ask to spread the word both on their blog and on social media sites is a great way to attract your first wave of links.

The second step is releasing the results. Combine the release with some nice visualization and a bit of controversy, and you've got yourself a fantastic piece of linkbait.

Microsites

Creating fun, quirky microsites is a great way to attract links. While some people might naturally link to your main site to give credit, they'll most likely link to the microsite, which should have at least one link back to you on it. One classic example is pointblankseo.com/book/microsites. If you're thinking they might be too big of an investment, know that they don't have to be fancy.

Google Maps Mashup

Google Maps is a great tool, and you can use it to attract links if you get it in front of the right audience. A great idea would be to map out all the industry events taking place this year.

For example, Mashable linked out to 100 helpful mashups in this post: pointblankseo.com/book/mashups.

Curated Rankings/Scores

If you create rankings or scores of people, companies, or anything else, and if it's decent enough, then trust us, you'll get a few links. The best part is that they don't even have to be accurate (of course it would be great if they were).

For example, visit Klout.com and this list of Top Blogs on Startups at topblogs.onstartups.com. Again, both aren't exactly accurate (Klout isn't the best depiction of your influence on Twitter, and the #1 blog on that list is no longer active), but people care about numbers and rankings, especially the ones that make them look good.

Crowdsourcing

Getting answers from a group of industry experts is another fantastic way to attract links. If the piece is good enough, and if you have the right influencers involved, the amount of links you'll attract can grow exponentially. This is because your contributors will do the promotion for you.

SEOmoz did a study on ranking factors, getting input from more than 130 different experts. You can read about it online at pointblankseo.com/book/factors. You can probably guess it was a huge success. It's attracted more than 27,000 links from more than 3,300 root domains.

Petitions

If you and your community are passionate about a certain issue, start a petition. If you can gain any traction from an industry news site, it could catch on like wildfire.

A petition on ec-petition.eu received more than 1,100 links from more than 200 root domains.

Note: Although not recommended, because it isn't hosted on your site, one option is to use Change.org to start your petition. It has an easy setup process, and because it's hosted on their already popular site, you get all the added benefits of professionalism and exposure.

Lists

1. People.
2. Love.
3. Lists!

Why? Because the content is super easy to digest.

This simple list of water conservation tips received more than 1,900 links from more than 400 root domains: pointblankseo.com/book/list.

Debunking Myths

If there's a common misconception in your industry, make sure you let everyone know. If it's big enough, and if your statements are bold enough, you could get some serious attention.

This debunking of 9/11 myths attracted more than 4,000 links from more than 200 root domains: pointblankseo.com/book/debunk.

Data/Research

By collecting data on just about anything, you can attract links. Why? Because, like lists, people absolutely love data. One reason is because they like to make conclusions from it that support their arguments.

TIP

If your data supports a side of an argument (i.e., nature vs. nurture debate), reach out to those that it would support. People love telling the world how right they are.

Take it one step further. Release it as straight data, then release it again in a way that makes it visually appealing.

This study on sexual harassment in grade school attracted more than 1,000 links from 125 root domains: pointblankseo.com/book/data.

Troll Bait (Controversy)

Troll bait is a great term. While we are not sure who coined the term first, it's a better way to say, "Create something controversial."

Remember Godaddy's SOPA fiasco? They originally supported SOPA (which stirred controversy), but then they stated they would now oppose it (which stirred even more controversy).

WARNING

Creating controversy for the sake of controversy is a dangerous game. If the opportunity presents itself, go for it, but don't go in cold looking just to create controversy; people can see right through it.

Interviews

Interviewing industry experts will always be a fantastic way to attract links, but getting them to interview is only half the battle. The other half is asking great questions.

A good way to find out what questions you should ask is by holding a Q&A with your blog's community, whether it's on Google+, Twitter, or any other site. Ask what kinds of questions your readers want to see answered.

Mixergy.com is home to more than 600 interviews, and more than a few have over 100 links.

HELPING WEBMASTERS

One of our personal favorite link-building strategies is helping out, or adding value to, webmasters. By doing something for them, they'll be much, much more likely to give you a link. Here are a few ways to help out webmasters.

Broken Links

Out of all the strategies listed, this is our favorite. The scalability of finding broken links is astounding. In a nutshell, you'll be finding pages that could potentially link to you, looking for broken links on the page, and if there are any, you'll let the webmaster know and ask if the broken link could be replaced with a link to you.

Fixing Grammar/Spelling

It's just as simple as it sounds: Look for grammar and spelling mistakes, notify the webmaster, and ask for a link on a relevant page.

Filling Gaps in Content

If a site is missing information on a certain topic, whether it's an article entirely or a portion of one that should be better elaborated on, reach out to the webmaster and ask if you could help fill that gap. Of course, ask for a link in the article in return.

Update Old Content

If information is out of date, do webmasters a favor and help update it for them. If you're in a rapidly changing industry such as SEO, look for articles and posts written a few years back that still get traffic (i.e., rank high for a decent keyword). This is because if many people no longer see the content, the webmaster probably won't care enough to have it updated.

Remember, when you do update the content, make sure you add a link to you in it.

Dead Content Recreation

Take broken links one step further by recreating the content found at those URLs, then outreaching to not only that specific linking site, but also other sites linking to that broken URL.

For this, use Archive.org to find what content used to be found at that URL.

Logo/Graphic/Web Design

A decent website usually has some sort of logo, graphic, and web design. If you have any experience with any of these, reach out to webmasters and ask if they'd like any of the above services at no cost.

Sometimes it doesn't have to be a major website makeover. Michael Kovis has helped me make a few CSS tweaks in the past, something that I've been very, very thankful for.

If you don't know design, you can get someone on Fiverr.com to create a logo for five dollars. No, it's not going to be amazing, but it'll get the job done.

Finding Malware

Use ScrapeBox to find sites with malware, reach out to those webmasters, let them know, and ask for a link. There are other ways to find malware, but Scrapebox is pretty handy for this.

> **WARNING**
>
> Don't go to an infected site to get contact information for its webmaster! You might get a virus. Use a whois look up such as whois.net to find contact info.

Fight Viagra Hackers

There's a huge issue on the internet that I didn't realize could be used to build links until recently. Hackers (most notably trying to get links with anchors like "buy cheap viagra") are infiltrating blogs, college sites, and regular html websites in order to get the links they want. A lot of times, the webmasters of these sites have no idea it's happening.

Find sites that have been hacked, let the webmaster know (a lot of times they honestly don't know it's happened) and tell them how to make the quick fix, then ask for a link or two once you've helped them out. Ninety-nine times out of a hundred they'd be more than happy to.

PAID STRATEGIES

If you have a little room in your budget, then consider some of the below paid strategies. Google is against paid links, but there are some out there that are acceptable, such as most of the ones listed below.

Paid Reviews

If you've got a product or service you want reviewed on a blog, you can pay for one. By using sites like SponsoredReviews.com, ReviewMe.com, and PayPerPost.com, you can pay for blogger reviews. Of course, they'll link to you in the review.

It's not exactly white hat, but it's something to at least be aware of.

Pay Authorities to Embed Your Badges

It's a paid link that cannot be detected, it increases brand awareness and trust, and best of all, it can be used to get natural embeds.

For example, if you get one of the two bloggers in the industry to embed a badge of "Featured in Top 10 X Blogs in 2012" on their blogs and you outreach to a few mid-level bloggers that you also included (exactly for this reason), they'd be more than happy to embed it, because if the big-time blogger did, they'd be honored to.

Honestly, if you're going to pay for a sitewide, this is the way to go. There are so many added bonuses.

And just in case you're wondering, this isn't white hat.

Note: If you go for spammy anchor text, and not branded or partial, it could send spam signals, so don't play around there.

Sponsor Contests

Blogging contests usually don't cost more than 50 to 100 dollars to sponsor. Make sure to look for ones that require participants to post about the contest on their blog and link to each of the sponsors in the post.

Sponsor Clubs

Most colleges have a wide range of clubs, and if you ask one to sponsor it for a link in return, they'll probably say yes. You can usually sponsor one for $50.

Sponsor Events

Whether it's a local meetup, industry conference, or anything in between, event groups are always looking for sponsors, and you can usually get a link in return for a 100- to 200-dollar sponsorship.

TIP

The moment the event is over, ask if you could sponsor next year's. The event committee will be so excited that they'd instantly say yes, and in the end you get the link for close to two years instead of one.

Donate to Charities and Nonprofits

Charities and nonprofit organizations almost always have a donors page. The amount you need to donate to get the link should be between $50 and $100.

Crowdfunding

While only some link out to funders, there are a ton of crowdfunding opportunities that you can use to make small investments in various businesses. For link building, make sure you get in touch with the individual business so you make sure that you can get a link in return for funding their project.

Sponsor Animal Shelters

There are usually more than a few local animal shelters you can sponsor, and sometimes the sponsorship (for a link) can be as low as $10.

Buying StumbleUpon Traffic for the Webmaster

Ask webmasters if they'd give you a link on a relevant page in exchange for between $10 and $20 worth of StumbleUpon Paid Discovery traffic. Sometimes they'd be willing to link regardless of the PD traffic, so this just encourages them to link even more.

Hire Industry Veterans

Relationship building can be hard. Find people in the industry you can hire who can tap into their list of contacts for links, because they've already built up those connections. This can be extremely helpful for those who are just starting out in an industry.

Hire Veteran Link Builders

Just like industry veterans, experienced link builders have built up little black books of contacts (at least the good ones have). Chances are they've dealt with people in either your vertical or a very similar one. In that case, they can get in touch with those contacts, saving you the time to initially build those relationships.

COLLEGE/EDUCATIONAL LINKS

.Edu links are some of the best, yet toughest links to get. Here are a few specific strategies that work great if you're willing to try them out.

Write Curriculum

Reach out to universities and let them know about your expertise. By writing curriculum for courses (the more basic, the easier it is to get involved), you can get a few citation links from their site.

Intern/Job Postings

If you have any job or internship opportunities, you can get a few easy .edu links. For those looking for an example, if you work in anthropology and you're looking for an intern, here's an easy link: pointblankseo.com/book/intern.

Offer Discounts

By offering discounts to faculty, teachers, and students, you can easily get links from pages like this: pointblankseo.com/book/discount.

Speak at Universities

Most universities announce speakers on their website, and when they do, make sure a link to your site is included.

Scholarships

Scholarships can become the bread and butter of your .edu link strategy if it's in the budget. Give out a decent-size scholarship, such as $500 or $1,000, and reach out to multiple colleges and high schools. You don't have to settle for just a couple here; usually there's not a limit on this one.

You could take it one step further and set it up as a contest; the finalists have to write blog posts on your blog on why they deserve it, and half the voting is done socially (i.e., tweets, +1s, Facebook Likes, and so forth). Heck, you could probably get even more creative at that point.

Alumni Directories

Most colleges dedicate a part of their site to their alumni, and some of them link out to their alumni's websites.

For example, a client's competitors had a link from one of the Harvard Business School's most authoritative pages, only because they got listed under "HBS Entrepreneurs." No, you probably didn't graduate from Harvard, but an edu link is an edu link.

Student Blogs

Students are allowed to create blogs on their respective college websites, so get in touch with them. They're a lot easier to get links from than a regular college webmaster. Whether it's buying them lunch or making sure you get a link from a college intern, you can always get links through students.

COMMUNITY STRATEGIES

By interacting in communities, not only can you build links, but also relationships (remember how important they are?). This is a great way to get to know people in your industry while snagging a few links at the same time.

Community Newspapers

There are a number of online newspapers that are run by the people, for the people. By contributing, curating, and adding your insight, you can get links from these sites on a regular basis (you get the chance to promote yourself in your bio on most of them).

Here are a few for example:

- Nowpublic.com
- Allvoices.com
- Demotix.com
- International.ohmynews.com
- Orato.com

Blog Commenting

It's definitely classified as low-hanging fruit, but you can still get value from commenting on blogs. To get the most value, comment on relevant blogs, do-follow blogs (blogs that offer followed links to their commenters), and CommentLuv blogs (blogs that have the CommentLuv plugin installed).

If you do it right, you'll build rapport with bloggers and links at the same time.

Forum Posting

Forum posting is a great way to find the people in your industry that are really passionate about your niche. Again, you'll get links when you post in the right forums.

Q&A

Using sites like Yahoo! Answers, you can build a few no-follow links that should also send a bit of traffic to your site. Make sure to cite pages on your site when answering questions in order to guarantee a link.

COMMUNITY PROJECTS

Interacting in communities is one subset of strategies, but why not create your own?

Creating a new project in your niche not only can help build your authority and trust, but it can also get you a few links if you know where to put them. Here are a few examples of what you could create.

New Online Community

Whether it's a niche forum, Q&A site, or social network, you can probably create it without much trouble.

A few options are vBulletin or Simple Press for a forum, Buddy Press for a social network, or qHub for a Q&A site.

If you want to go above and beyond the call of duty, create a community from scratch. Inbound.org, created by Rand Fishkin and Dharmesh Shah, is exactly that.

Wiki

Wikis are great, but only if you get people involved. Having a little influence to begin with helps a ton. By outreaching to influencers to contribute and by incentivizing contributions, you can build it up as an authority. Again, make sure to link to yourself with it.

Industry-Specific Directory

Creating a human-curated, quality niche directory is something worth looking into if there isn't one in your industry. If the design looks like every other directory and the submissions you're accepting are subpar, you'll have little success, but if you're accepting only quality sites, it could get listed often on resource lists.

Start with directory software, then customizing from there. Just Google "directory software" if you're looking for one; most don't cost more than $100. Obviously, since this is a link-building strategy, link to your main site.

LEVERAGE EXISTING OPPORTUNITIES

Chances are there are links out there that are already yours that you just haven't gotten yet. For example, if someone uses your content, you should be able to get a link back. Here are a few existing opportunities for you to snag a link or two.

Asking Customers

If someone just bought something from you, then this is the perfect time to ask for a link if they have any influence online. Ask them to write a review of your product or service, and then offer to help promote it to spread the word. It's a win-win!

Contacting People Using Your Images/Infographics

By using Google's reverse image search, you can easily find other websites using your images or infographics. Politely outreach to each and ask if you could have a link back for using them. If they don't, make sure to let them know it's copyright infringement to use your copyrighted images without permission.

Brand Mentions

If your brand gets mentioned on the web, then make sure you ask for a link. For example, if someone mentioned "Point Blank SEO" on their blog, I might ask if they could include a link so the reader would know where Point Blank SEO is located on the web. You can easily set up free alerts with tools like Google Alerts to find who's talking about your brand.

Associations/Organizations

If you're a part of an association or organization, chances are they have a website. If they do, find out if they link out to their members. Get included if they do.

Link Re-Purposing

If you've got too many links with generic or branded anchor text, reach out to those webmasters and ask if they could alter the anchor text to either exact or partial match. You could also do just the opposite if unnatural link signals are hurting you.

Reclaiming Twitter Links

People will sometimes link to your Twitter account, so take advantage. You can do this by going to the Twitter widget page (pointblankseo.com/book/widget), building a full-page-size widget and placing it on its own page, then asking webmasters to link to that page rather than directly to Twitter.

If you're still confused, you can find a guide online at: pointblankseo.com/twitter.

Previous Linkers

If someone has linked to you in the past, chances are they might be willing to link to you in the future. Get to know them, and make sure they're up to date with your content, because that only leads to more links.

Try using Linkstant.com to instantly see who's linked to you. Make sure to stop by those sites and leave a thank-you comment.

Your Influence

If you've built up influence, you can definitely use this to build links. If I got an email from Aaron Wall asking to review his toolset on my blog, I'd be more than willing to.

Outside of outreach, you can use your influence for a ton of things. For example, Ann Smarty used her influence to get a chance to write posts for Mashable (no lack of quality links there).

In general, you can use your influence to get a much higher success rate with every other strategy explored in this book, but remember: If the person you're contacting doesn't know who you are, then your influence is worthless (e.g., a .gov webmaster couldn't care less if you're a big-shot travel blogger).

Reclaim Links Pointing to 404s

Sometimes links to your website break over time, whether it's because you've moved the intended page, or because the webmaster messed up your URL. Go into Google Webmaster Tools to see which pages are getting 404 errors, then redirect those pages to either the homepage or the implied intended page.

GIVE

You have something that people want, so give it away. Here's a list of things you can give to get links.

Products to Bloggers

There's no better way to connect with bloggers than by giving them your product or service in exchange for a review. Usually there are a lot of mid-level bloggers in big industries more than willing to, so this can be quite scalable.

Free Ebooks/Products Using Social Payment Systems

Give out free e-books and products using services like PayWithATweet.com or Cloudflood.com. In order to get it, you have to tweet or share it, thus causing a landslide of social shares.

No, there's no guarantee you'll get a link, but it's a great way to get your stuff in front of a lot of potential linkers' eyes.

Note: Don't forget to submit those e-books to e-book directories!

Discounts and Coupons

Giving out discounts and coupons is a great way to get mentions in lists like this one: pointblankseo.com/book/coupons. Make sure to reach out to writers who dedicate posts to discounts and coupons; usually they'd be more than happy to include your offers.

Social Coupons

Sites like Living Social and Groupon allow you to include anchor text links in the description of your coupons. If you're wondering, Google does cache the pages, so we're 99 percent sure these links are indexed.

Contest Giveaways

If you have a product or service, and if there's a relevant blogging contest taking place, reach out to the blogger running it and ask if you could give your product or service to the winner. They'd be more than happy to, and they'll give you a link on the contest page if you ask.

DEVELOP RELATIONSHIPS

Links and relationships are directly related. The more bloggers and webmasters you know, the more links you'll get. Here are a few great ways to build relationships.

Random Acts of Kindness

Whenever you can, be nice to people. Always be on the lookout for helping those in need. This isn't exactly an actionable strategy for link building, but you'd be surprised. These random acts can turn into lasting relationships.

Give a Crap

Actually care about people. Show them you're not just a bot with a picture, but that you're somewhat human. If they share on Twitter that their daughter just graduated, congratulate them. Something as simple as that can open up your chances to build a relationship in the future.

Participate

If someone is conducting a survey or testing something, get involved and participate. Those are great chances to start conversations with new people.

Local Meetups

Whether you find one or start one, meetups are a fantastic way to get to know people close by. For example, if you live in a big city (Seattle, NYC, Philly) then meetups are absolutely perfect. I highly recommend Meetup.com if you're looking to find or start one.

User Group Meetups

A great way to get to know people who think like you is by finding those who use the same products or services you do. A great example is the Hubspot User Group Summit.

Conferences

Seriously, go to them. At the time I'm writing this, I've only gone to one, but it was awesome and I highly recommend it.

Call Them

Yep, I said it. Get them on the phone. Make your contacts hear your voice and know that you're a real person.

Ben Wills was the first to do this with me. I now know a lot more about him and Ontolo (his toolset), something I'm extremely grateful for.

Twitter RTs, @s, and DMs

If you want to get to know someone on Twitter, first retweet them a few times. Then respond a couple times to a few of their tweets, then continue the conversation as direct messages. Finally, ask to email (because 140 characters is never enough), and now you've got the ball rolling.

Answer Questions

Answer questions on Twitter, Quora, and anywhere else people hang out. People ask questions all the time, so being at the right place at the right time by helping them out will definitely put you on their radar.

TRAFFIC DRIVERS

Not all links that we build are for search rankings. Some are for traffic. We are getting high rankings so we get more traffic, right? Besides, having all your eggs (links) in one basket (Google) is never a good idea. Here are a few examples of links for traffic.

Newsletters

Including links back to your site in newsletters is a great way to get traffic, but take it one step further. Find influential newsletters in your niche and try to get a link included. For example, I've gotten a link in Eric Ward's *Link Moses Private*. An even bigger target (that could potentially crash my site) in our industry is the *Moz Top 10* newsletter, which has 220,000 subscribers. Yeah. I know.

TIP

Find out who's sending out the newsletters, and get to know them.

Email Signatures

If you send out 100 emails a day, having an email signature with a link back can drive an extra 50+ people a day to your website. It's not much, but it requires zero effort.

LOCAL

Based on where you're located, you can get a few links from local websites. Here are a few ways to use your location to build links.

Better Business Bureau

We don't often suggest an individual site, but when we do, it's the Better Business Bureau. This link will pass more trust than almost any other link in your profile. The price is determined by state/region/city and by number of employees. The St. Louis BBB ranges from $370 for one to three employees all the way to $865+ for 100 to 200 employees. Anything over that, as well as additional websites, incurs as additional charges.

That being said, you are supposed to get a "do-follow" link out of all this. You need to check on your listing once it is published as each region has their own rules regarding their directory of businesses. There have been some instances where your business's website URL in the directory listing was *not* a live link, only text. All you have to do is contact your BBB representative and ask for that to be changed.

Chamber of Commerce

Getting a link from your chamber of commerce is a guaranteed link just waiting for you to get. In some cases, though, it takes a little bit of time to find the right person to get in touch with.

Local Listings

Submit your site to local listings. Here's a fantastic list created by Peter Attia of all the best sites for this: pointblankseo.com/book/local.

Another example is Yelp.com.

Library

Most local libraries have a website, and most of them have somewhat of a link profile. Nonetheless, get in touch, and do what you can to get a link; it's going to be a link from one of the most white hat sites in your profile.

LINKING OUT

Linking out is a great way to build links, because when bloggers see they've been linked to by your blog (along with 50 visitors coming over from that post), they'll at the very least check out your content, if not tweet and link to it.

Why? Because people are much more likely to help out others that have helped out them. This is the exact same idea as helping out webmasters in the strategies I listed above.

Getting Trackbacks

As opposed to giving trackbacks, find blogs that allow you to get trackback links. For example, the Google blog gives out trackback links, and even though they're no-follow, they're still worth something.

Link Roundups

Whether they're monthly, weekly, or even daily, doing roundups of great posts in your niche is a fantastic way to put you on the map. Mid-level, and even some high-level, bloggers take notice when they get links from these.

TIP

Make sure you add a little insight to why you listed the post. It helps the bloggers being linked to know that someone is actually taking the time to read their posts.

Giving Trackbacks

Reward people who link to you by giving trackback links. Take it one step further and make them do-follow. When they sort through their backlinks and see these, they'll be a lot more likely to link out to you in the future.

Active Medium-Level Bloggers

Medium-level bloggers are the best audiences to target. When they get linked to, they go bananas (I did when I got my first few links!).

Linking out and letting them know you did so is a great strategy for this large group. Usually the best natural link profiles come from blogs that have control over this middle group.

Mention Specific People Whenever Possible

Whenever possible (and we mean whenever possible!), mention specific people. People love getting mentioned. Link to their site (so they know they got mentioned), and when they find out, they're usually more than willing to share the post at the very least (if not link to it!). Again, this is a great way to put yourself on their map.

Linker Outreach

Find people on Delicious.com, or other social sharing sites that have saved similar content to yours, outreach to them, letting them know about your content (i.e., an upcoming infographic), and let them do the rest; they'll share it or link to it if they like it.

Relevant Reciprocal Links

Yep, I included it. If you're going to exchange (reciprocate) links with a website, don't do it as if you're living in 1998. Make sure they're the most relevant, trustworthy websites you've ever come across. If they're not, don't do it.

Second-Tier Link Building

Building links to pages that link to you can be awesome if you do it right. You not only can pass more juice back to your site, but you can also use it for reputation management and to drive sales.

> **TIP**
>
> Do second-tier link building to trustworthy sites linking to you, such as a guest post on a highly authoritative blog. For example, if you're doing some broken link building, asking for the replacement link to be to a highly trustworthy site will get you accepted a lot more often than if you asked for a link to you.
>
> This is because the site is more trustworthy (webmaster is more willing to link) and because you're not asking for a link to the domain that hosts your email (i.e., jcooper@pointblankseo.com asking for a link to pointblankseo.com), meaning it looks more natural in the eyes of the webmaster.

Networking

Use some of the relationships you've built to create a network of similar noncompeting blogs. Link out to them, and ask them to do the same. A good number to have in your network is five; it's not too much, but it's not too little.

For example, make sure everyone links out to each different blog in the network once a month. Heck, make it once a week.

It's like reciprocal linking, but way better, because the links are relevant, contextual, and natural in Google's eyes.

Help a Reporter Out (HARO)

HARO, or Help a Reporter Out, connects journalists with bloggers & industry experts. By becoming a source, you can get big-time links from news sites.

From personal experience, this is one of the best ways to get high-quality press mentions without much work.

PR Outreach

Good ol' fashioned PR outreach is always a great idea if you're buzzworthy. If you're not up for hiring a PR company for this, make sure you research who you're pitching, and make sure to keep it short and to the point. If you do it right, you'll build up a relationship with the person you're pitching long before you pitch them. This will also result in you being able to tap into that relationship multiple times, and not for just a one-off pitch.

> **TIP**
>
> Take things one step further. If you write something up for a news publication, ask if you could regularly contribute by creating a weekly column. If they say yes, then you've just landed yourself a fantastic long-term link opportunity.

Top Commentators Widget

Some blogs have a top commentators widget that displays the top commentators in the sidebar of their blog. All you have to do is make it up on that leaderboard and you'll get a sitewide link. Granted, it might take 10 to 15 comments, it's still worth it.

Make sure you don't drop all the comments on the same day; you'd look like an idiot. Do one or two a day for a couple of weeks until you get that link.

CONCLUSION

There will always be a new strategy or two every once in a while, but this list should keep you for quite some time.

As time passes, understand that some of these strategies will be thrown out as new algorithm updates are introduced, so always keep up with the latest search engine news, whether you read it by scanning the press, reading SEO blogs, or subscribing to a newsletter.

Chapter 26

Epilogue

The web moves quickly. During the time we've been writing this book, hundreds of updates have been made to Google's algorithm. Some of the better-known changes have names, like Panda and Penguin. You can find thousands of blog posts, articles, and columns about these and many other algorithmic updates just by doing a few Google searches for them. But beyond the changes that make their way into the SEO community's consciousness, it's important to remember the overall purpose of these changes in the first place: to improve the search results for end users, to root out spam and link schemes. And I applaud Google for it. For Google and other search engines, this means constantly evaluating and reevaluating the hundreds of signals they use when examining content, links, and web pages.

As the engines get smarter, one of the unfortunate downsides is the amount of bad information that finds its way into the mainstream SEO community. Making decisions based on bad information can cost you dearly. After seeing so many companies waste large sums of money chasing poorly thought-out linking strategies, about a year ago I began a private strategy service called LinkMoses Private, which is a play on my industry nickname (I'm a notorious white hatter). LinkMoses Private is designed to teach you linking techniques that help with both click traffic and organic rankings today and for the long term. The ultimate goal of LinkMoses Private is to help you improve and sculpt a more effective inbound link profile. This involves recognizing the wide variety of linking opportunities that are available to you, from social media to the deep web, if you know where to look and how to pursue them. If you've read this far, I encourage you to visit http://www.ericward.com/linkmosesprivate.html. There you can take the next step toward creating the most effective inbound link profile possible.

Resources

Rather than build a glossary from the terms in our book, we decided to list various SEO glossaries as definitions vary. The following can help you better understand the world of link building.

LINK BUILDING AND SEO GLOSSARIES

- www.linkbuildingwiki.com/wiki/Link_Building_-_Glossary
- www.seobook.com/glossary/
- www.seomoz.org/blog/smwc-and-other-essential-seo-jargon
- www.seo-theory.com/seo-glossary/
- www.sempo.org/?page=glossary
- pageonepower.com/link-building-glossary/
- searchenginewatch.com/page/glossary
- www.kunocreative.com/blog/bid/66998/The-Inbound-Marketers-Link-Building-SEO-Glossary

Index